RASHOMON

AND OTHER STORIES

BY

RYUNOSUKE AKUTAGAWA

TRANSLATED BY TAKASHI KOJIMA

INTRODUCTION BY HOWARD HIBBET

CHARLES E. TUTTLE COMPANY

TOKYO, JAPAN

Published in Japan by
the Charles E. Tuttle Company, Inc.
of Rutland, Vermont & Tokyo, Japan

Editorial offices:
Suido 1-chome, 2-6,
Bunkyo-ku, Tokyo

First edition, January 1952
Two subsequent reprintings
Second edition, January 1954
Twenty-third printing, 1997

ISBN 0-8048-1457-0
Printed in Singapore

PREFACE

The six stories of this collection were chosen with the aim of presenting Akutagawa's finest and most representative writings. Only one of them (*Rashō-mon*) has appeared in an earlier translation.

I wish to express my thanks to the following persons, for their kind assistance, and for their many valuable suggestions and criticisms: Mr. C. G. Wells, Chief Writer of the Far East Network; Mr. Walter E. Morgan, Chief of the School Administration and Finance Branch, CIE, SCAP; Mr. Harold Gosling and Mr. John Rockard, correspondents of the British Commonwealth Public Relations; Mr. Richard B. Farnsworth, formerly of CIE, SCAP; and Lieutenant D. L. Donohugh, formerly of the Press Advisory Division, SCAP.

TAKASHI KOJIMA

Tokyo, Japan.

CONTENTS

INTRODUCTION

To sketch the background and temperament of Akutagawa Ryūnosuke is to risk a melancholy cliché. He was brilliant, sensitive, cynical, neurotic; he lived in Tokyo, went to the University, taught briefly, and joined the literary staff of a newspaper. Even his early suicide (in 1927, at thirty-five) only heightens the portrait of a modern Japanese intellectual, the double victim of an unsympathetic society and a split culture. But it is a vague composite portrait. For Akutagawa himself, aloof, elusive, individual, remains withdrawn behind the polished facade of his collected works. All that needs to be known about their author, besides the name stamped on the binding, may be found within these poems, essays, miscellaneous writings, and more than a hundred beautifully finished stories.

The stories have a dazzling and perhaps deceptive sheen. Superficial critics called Akutagawa precious, or decadent, or dismissed him as a fatiguingly clever dilettante. Unprepared for the strength of his later satires, they supposed him to care only for the superb texture of his prose. Translation protects us from the seductions of this style, yet encourages a similar error, since the nuances of Akutagawa's prose are what conveys the essence of his thought. Like Natsume Sōseki and Mori Ōgai, whom he admired, Akutagawa used his language delicately, precisely, and with a

9

richness enhanced by a knowledge of several litera-
tures. It is significant that his first published writings
were translations of Yeats and Anatole France. He
remarked once that words must yield more than the
bare dictionary meanings; he had a poet's feeling for
their shapes and flavors, as well as their ambiguities,
and he combined them with such freshness and eco-
nomy that his phrasing never lacks distinction. Like
Picasso, Akutagawa often varied his style, but always,
whatever the particular blend of vernacular and man-
darin, he controlled it with scrupulous precision. A
master of tone, he gave his stories a cool classic surface, colored but never marred by the wit and warmth
underlying that perfect glaze. The composure of his
style is undisturbed even by vivid accents of the sordid
or the bizarre.

Detachment was a key strategy to Akutagawa.
As a narrator, he liked to be unseen, impersonal; he
cultivated the oblique glance. When he did enter his
stories, it was usually in the slight role of the observer
or the suave self-effacing compiler. Old tales and
legends, historical settings of the remote Heian Period
or the feudal ages which followed—these he used not
to turn his elaborate erudition to account, but to
enrich and extend the implications of his themes, and
to maintain aesthetic distance. The early era of
Christian conversion in Japan, in the sixteenth cen-
tury, was a favorite of his; in *Hōkyōnin no shi* (*The
Martyr*) he exploited it to the point of hoax by sup-
porting an archaic style with a source reference which,

after an interval for learned controversy, he acknowl-
edged to be fictitious. It suited his ironic taste to play
the illusionist who leaves his audience staring blankly
into a mirror.

But Akutagawa did more than deceive scholars
and baffle the unwary: he antagonized ruling critical
opinion. His attention to style, his preference for
techniques of indirection and restraint, his indiffer-
ence to current dogma—such attitudes were heresy
to both the leading literary schools. The Proletarian
writers, flourishing in the '20's, found nothing in
common between Akutagawa's subtle stories and their
own carefully chosen but grossly cut slices-of-life.
The Naturalists, their rivals, had moved toward
romantic individualism, forgetting Zola's concept of
social inquiry. Dominant since the Russo-Japanese
War, they sanctioned only the literary method to
which, in the name of the first-person-singular *shi-
shōsetsu*, their successors still adhere. This was the
Confession, ranging from the sentimental memoir to
the clinical report of an author's sexual life. Despite
the exhaustion of the autobiographical form of fiction
after Proust, these novelists went on eagerly probing
their wounds and laying themselves open to reproach;
while Akutagawa, unmoved by the exhibition of so
many tedious egos, went his own way. A few of his
stories suggest maliciously that confession itself may
be false. *Yabu no naka* (*In a Grove*), for example,
converts an old melodramatic tale into a series of
conflicting statements which undermine our prosaic

11

confidence in distinguishing between subjective and objective, truth and fiction. Even the dark testaments which he left before suicide contain flashes of mockery to perplex the straightforward reader.

There are enough Swiftian touches in Akutagawa to show his hatred of stupidity, greed, hypocrisy, and the rising jingoism of the day. But Akutagawa's artistic integrity kept him from joining his contemporaries in easy social criticism or naive introspection. If, too often, his finely enameled miniatures seem cold, over-subtilized, worn thin by an obsessive critical sense, still they are never merely decorative. What he did was to question the values of his society, dramatize the complexities of human psychology, and study, with a Zen taste for paradox, the precarious balance of illusion and reality. He developed a variety of techniques—from realism to fantasy, symbolism to surrealism—and used all of them in the search for poetic truth. Akutagawa was both intellectual and artist, and it was the quality of his artistry that enabled him to explore these difficult problems as deeply as he did, and to give his perceptions such exquisite and durable form.

HOWARD HIBBETT

Tokyo, 1951

IN A GROVE

Testimony of a Woodcutter before a High Police Commissioner

Yes, sir. Certainly, it was I who found the body. This morning, as usual, I went to cut my daily quota of cedars, when I found the body in a grove in a hollow in the mountains. The exact location? About 150 meters off the Yamashina stage road. It's an out-of-the-way grove of bamboo and cedars.

The body was lying flat on its back dressed in a bluish silk kimono and a wrinkled head-dress of the Kyoto style. A single sword-stroke had pierced the breast. The fallen bamboo-blades around it were stained with bloody blossoms. No, the blood was no longer running. The wound had dried up, I believe. And also, a gad-fly was stuck fast there, hardly noticing my footsteps.

You ask me if I saw a sword or any such thing?

No, nothing, sir. I found only a rope at the root of a cedar near by. And...well, in addition to a rope, I found a comb. That was all. Apparently he must have made a battle of it before he was murdered, because the grass and fallen bamboo-blades had been trampled down all around.

"A horse was near by?"

No, sir. It's hard enough for a man to enter, let alone a horse.

TESTIMONY OF A TRAVELING BUDDHIST PRIEST BEFORE THE HIGH POLICE COMMISSIONER

The time? Certainly, it was about noon yesterday, sir. The unfortunate man was on the road from Sekiyama to Yamashina. He was walking toward Sekiyama with a woman accompanying him on horseback, who I have since learned was his wife. A scarf hanging from her head hid her face from view. All I saw was the color of her clothes, a lilac-colored suit. Her horse was a sorrel with a fine mane. The lady's height? Oh, about four feet five inches. Since I am a Buddhist priest, I took little notice about her details. Well, the man was armed with a sword as well as a bow and arrows. And I remember that he carried some twenty odd arrows in his quiver.

Little did I expect that he would meet such a fate. Truly human life is as evanescent as the morning dew or a flash of lightning. My words are inadequate to express my sympathy for him.

TESTIMONY OF A POLICEMAN BEFORE THE HIGH POLICE COMMISSIONER

The man that I arrested? He is a notorious brigand called Tajomaru. When I arrested him, he had fallen off his horse. He was groaning on the bridge at Awataguchi. The time? It was in the early hours of last night. For the record, I might say that the other day I tried to arrest him, but un-

fortunately he escaped. He was wearing a dark blue
silk kimono and a large plain sword. And, as you
see, he got a bow and arrows somewhere. You say
that this bow and these arrows look like the ones
owned by the dead man? Then Tajomaru must be
the murderer. The bow wound with leather strips,
the black lacquered quiver, the seventeen arrows with
hawk feathers—these were all in his possession I
believe. Yes, sir, the horse is, as you say, a sorrel
with a fine mane. A little beyond the stone bridge
I found the horse grazing by the roadside, with his
long rein dangling. Surely there is some providence
in his having been thrown by the horse.

Of all the robbers prowling around Kyoto, this
Tajomaru has given the most grief to the women in
town. Last autumn a wife who came to the mountain
back of the Pindora of the Toribe Temple, presumably to pay a visit, was murdered, along with a girl.
It has been suspected that it was his doing. If this
criminal murdered the man, you cannot tell what he
may have done with the man's wife. May it please
your honor to look into this problem as well.

Testimony of an Old Woman before the High Police Commissioner

Yes, sir, that corpse is the man who married my
daughter. He does not come from Kyoto. He was
a samurai in the town of Kokufu in the province of
Wakasa. His name was Kanazawa no Takehiko, and

his age was twenty-six. He was of a gentle disposi-
tion, so I am sure he did nothing to provoke the anger
of others.

My daughter? Her name is Masago, and her
age is nineteen. She is a spirited, fun-loving girl,
but I am sure she has never known any man except
Takehiko. She has a small, oval, dark-complected
face with a mole at the corner of her left eye.

Yesterday Takehiko left for Wakasa with my
daughter. What bad luck it is that things should
have come to such a sad end! What has become of
my daughter? I am resigned to giving up my son-
in-law as lost, but the fate of my daughter worries me
sick. For heaven's sake leave no stone unturned to
find her. I hate that robber Tajomaru, or whatever
his name is. Not only my son-in-law, but my daughter
... (Her later words were drowned in tears.)

TAJOMARU'S CONFESSION

I killed him, but not her. Where's she gone? I
can't tell. Oh, wait a minute. No torture can make
me confess what I don't know. Now things have
come to such a head, I won't keep anything from you.

Yesterday a little past noon I met that couple.
Just then a puff of wind blew, and raised her hanging
scarf, so that I caught a glimpse of her face. Instantly it was again covered from my view. That may
have been one reason; she looked like a Bodhisattva.
At that moment I made up my mind to capture her

even if I had to kill her man.

Why? To me killing isn't a matter of such great consequence as you might think. When a woman is captured, her man has to be killed anyway. In killing, I use the sword I wear at my side. Am I the only one who kills people? You, you don't use your swords. You kill people with your power, with your money. Sometimes you kill them on the pretext of working for their good. It's true they don't bleed. They are in the best of health, but all the same you've killed them. It's hard to say who is a greater sinner, you or me. (An ironical smile.)

But it would be good if I could capture a woman without killing her man. So, I made up my mind to capture her, and do my best not to kill him. But it's out of the question on the Yamashina stage road. So I managed to lure the couple into the mountains.

It was quite easy. I became their traveling companion, and I told them there was an old mound in the mountain over there, and that I had dug it open and found many mirrors and swords. I went on to tell them I'd buried the things in a grove behind the mountain, and that I'd like to sell them at a low price to anyone who would care to have them. Then . . . you see, isn't greed terrible? He was beginning to be moved by my talk before he knew it. In less than half an hour they were driving their horse toward the mountain with me.

When he came in front of the grove, I told them that the treasures were buried in it, and I asked them to come and see. The man had no objection—he was blinded by greed. The woman said she would wait on horseback. It was natural for her to say so, at the sight of a thick grove. To tell you the truth, my plan worked just as I wished, so I went into the grove with him, leaving her behind alone.

The grove is only bamboo for some distance. About fifty yards ahead there's a rather open clump of cedars. It was a convenient spot for my purpose. Pushing my way through the grove, I told him a plausible lie that the treasures were buried under the cedars. When I told him this, he pushed his laborious way toward the slender cedar visible through the grove. After a while the bamboo thinned out, and we came to where a number of cedars grew in a row. As soon as we got there, I seized him from behind. Because he was a trained, sword-bearing warrior, he was quite strong, but he was taken by surprise, so there was no help for him. I soon tied him up to the root of a cedar. Where did I get a rope? Thank heaven, being a robber, I had a rope with me, since I might have to scale a wall at any moment. Of course it was easy to stop him from calling out by gagging his mouth with fallen bamboo leaves.

When I disposed of him, I went to his woman and asked her to come and see him, because he seemed to have been suddenly taken sick. It's needless to say that this plan also worked well. The woman, her sedge hat off, came into the depths of the grove,

18

where I led her by the hand. The instant she caught sight of her husband, she drew a small sword. I've never seen a woman of such violent temper. If I'd been off guard, I'd have got a thrust in my side. I dodged, but she kept on slashing at me. She might have wounded me deeply or killed me. But I'm Tajomaru. I managed to strike down her small sword without drawing my own. The most spirited woman is defenseless without a weapon. At last I could satisfy my desire for her without taking her husband's life.

Yes,... without taking his life. I had no wish to kill him. I was about to run away from the grove, leaving the woman behind in tears, when she frantically clung to my arm. In broken fragments of words, she asked that either her husband or I die. She said it was more trying than death to have her shame known to two men. She gasped out that she wanted to be the wife of whichever survived. Then a furious desire to kill him seized me. (Gloomy excitement.)

Telling you in this way, no doubt I seem a crueler man than you. But that's because you didn't see her face. Especially her burning eyes at that moment. As I saw her eye to eye, I wanted to make her my wife even if I were to be struck by lightning. I wanted to make her my wife... this single desire filled my mind. This was not only lust, as you might think. At that time if I'd had no other desire than lust, I'd surely not have minded knocking her down and running away. Then I wouldn't have stained my sword with his blood. But the moment I gazed at her face in the dark grove, I decided not to leave there without killing him.

But I didn't like to resort to unfair means to kill him. I untied him and told him to cross swords with me. (The rope that was found at the root of the cedar is the rope I dropped at the time.) Furious with anger, he drew his thick sword. And quick as thought, he sprang at me ferociously, without speaking a word. I needn't tell you how our fight turned out. The twenty-third stroke...please remember this. I'm impressed with this fact still. Nobody under the sun has ever clashed swords with me twenty strokes. (A cheerful smile.)

When he fell, I turned toward her, lowering my blood-tained sword. But to my great astonishment she was gone. I wondered to where she had run away. I looked for her in the clump of cedars. I listened, but heard only a groaning sound from the throat of the dying man.

As soon as we started to cross swords, she may have run away through the grove to call for help. When I thought of that, I decided it was a matter of life and death to me. So, robbing him of his sword, and bow and arrows, I ran out to the mountain road. There I found her horse still grazing quietly. It would be a mere waste of words to tell you the later details, but before I entered town I had already parted with the sword. That's all my confession. I know that my head will be hung in chains anyway, so put me down for the maximum penalty.   (A defiant attitude.)

Confession of a Woman Who Has Come to the *Shimizu* Temple

That man in the blue silk kimono, after forcing me to yield to him, laughed mockingly as he looked at my bound husband. How horrified my husband must have been! But no matter how hard he struggled in agony, the rope cut into him all the more tightly.   In spite of myself I ran stumblingly toward his side. Or rather I tried to run toward him, but the man instantly knocked me down.   Just at that moment I saw an indescribable light in my husband's eyes. Something beyond expression...his eyes make me shudder even now.   That instantaneous look of my husband, who couldn't speak a word, told me all his heart.   The flash in his eyes was neither anger nor sorrow...only a cold light, a look of loathing.   More struck by the look in his eyes than by the blow of the thief, I called out in spite of myself and fell unconscious.

In the course of time I came to, and found that the man in blue silk was gone.   I saw only my husband still bound to the root of the cedar.   I raised myself from the bamboo-blades with difficulty, and looked into his face; but the expression in his eyes was just the same as before.

Beneath the cold contempt in his eyes, there was

21

hatred. Shame, grief, and anger...I don't know how to express my heart at that time. Reeling to my feet, I went up to my husband.

"Takejiro," I said to him, "since things have come to this pass, I cannot live with you. I'm determined to die,...but you must die, too. You saw my shame. I can't leave you alive as you are."

This was all I could say. Still he went on gazing at me with loathing and contempt. My heart breaking, I looked for his sword. It must have been taken by the robber. Neither his sword nor his bow and arrows were to be seen in the grove. But fortunately my small sword was lying at my feet. Raising it over head, once more I said, "Now give me your life. I'll follow you right away."

When he heard these words, he moved his lips with difficulty. Since his mouth was stuffed with leaves, of course his voice could not be heard at all. But at a glance I understood his words. Despising me, his look said only, "Kill me." Neither conscious nor unconscious, I stabbed the small sword through the lilac-colored kimono into his breast.

Again at this time I must have fainted. By the time I managed to look up, he had already breathed his last—still in bonds. A streak of sinking sunlight streamed through the clump of cedars and bamboos, and shone on his pale face. Gulping down my sobs, I untied the rope from his dead body. And...and what has become of me since I have no more strength to tell you. Anyway I hadn't the strength to die. I stabbed my own throat with the small sword, I threw myself into a pond at the foot of the mountain, and I tried to kill myself in many ways. Unable to end my life, I am still living in dishonor. (A lonely smile.) Worthless as I am, I must have been forsaken even by the most merciful Kwannon. I killed my own husband. I was violated by the robber. Whatever can I do? Whatever can I...I...(Gradually, violent sobbing.)

STORY OF THE MURDERED MAN, AS TOLD THROUGH A MEDIUM

After violating my wife, the robber, sitting there, began to speak comforting words to her. Of course I couldn't speak. My whole body was tied fast to the root of a cedar. But meanwhile I winked at her many times, as much as to say "Don't believe the robber". I wanted to convey some such meaning to her. But my wife, sitting dejectedly on the bamboo leaves, was looking hard at her lap. To all appearance, she was listening to his words. I was agonized by jealousy. In the meantime the robber went on with his clever talk, from one subject to another. The robber finally made his bold, brazen proposal. "Once your virtue is stained, you won't get along well with your husband, so won't you be my wife instead? It's my love for you that made me be violent toward you."

While the criminal talked, my wife raised her

face as if in a trance. She had never looked so
beautiful as at that moment. What did my beautiful
wife say in answer to him while I was sitting bound
there? I am lost in space, but I have never thought
of her answer without burning with anger and jealousy. Truly she said,... "Then take me away with
you wherever you go."

This is not the whole of her sin. If that were all,
I would not be tormented so much in the dark. When
she was going out of the grove as if in a dream, her
hand in the robber's, she suddenly turned pale, and
pointed at me tied to the root of the cedar, and said,
"Kill him! I cannot marry you as long as he lives."
"Kill him!" she cried many times, as if she had gone
crazy. Even now these words threaten to blow me
headlong into the bottomless abyss of darkness. Has
such a hateful thing come out of a human mouth ever
before? Have such cursed words ever struck a
human ear, even once? Even once such a...(A
sudden cry of scorn.) At these words the robber
himself turned pale. "Kill him," she cried, clinging
to his arms. Looking hard at her, he answered neither yes nor no. ...but hardly had I thought about
his answer before she had been knocked down into
the bamboo leaves. (Again a cry of scorn.) Quietly
folding his arms, he looked at me and said, "What
will you do with her? Kill her or save her? You
have only to nod. Kill her?" For these words alone
I would like to pardon his crime.

While I hesitated, she shrieked and ran into the

depths of the grove. The robber instantly snatched at her, but he failed even to grasp her sleeve.

After she ran away, he took up my sword, and my bow and arrows. With a single stroke he cut one of my bonds. I remember his mumbling, "My fate is next." Then he disappeared from the grove. All was silent after that. No, I heard someone crying. Untying the rest of my bonds, I listened carefully, and I noticed that it was my own crying. (Long silence.)

I raised my exhausted body from the root of the cedar. In front of me there was shining the small sword which my wife had dropped. I took it up and stabbed it into my breast. A bloody lump rose to my mouth, but I didn't feel any pain. When my breast grew cold, everything was as silent as the dead in their graves. What profound silence! Not a single bird-note was heard in the sky over this grave in the hollow of the mountains. Only a lonely light lingered on the cedars and mountain. By and by the light gradually grew fainter, till the cedars and bamboo were lost to view. Lying there, I was enveloped in deep silence.

Then someone crept up to me. I tried to see who it was. But darkness had already been gathering round me. Someone...that someone drew the small sword softly out of my breast in its invisible hand. At the same time once more blood flowed into my mouth. And once and for all I sank down into the darkness of space.

RASHOMON*

It was a chilly evening. A servant of a samurai stood under the Rashōmon, waiting for a break in the rain.

No one else was under the wide gate. On the thick column, its crimson lacquer rubbed off here and there, perched a cricket. Since the Rashōmon stands on Sujaku Avenue, a few other people at least, in sedge hat or nobleman's headgear, might have been expected to be waiting there for a break in the rain storm. But no one was near except this man.

For the past few years the city of Kyōto had been visited by a series of calamities, earthquakes, whirlwinds, and fires, and Kyōto had been greatly devastated. Old chronicles say that broken pieces of Buddhist images and other Buddhist objects, with their lacquer, gold, or silver leaf worn off, were heaped up on roadsides to be sold as firewood. Such being the state of affairs in Kyōto, the repair of the Rashōmon was out of the question. Taking advantage of the devastation, foxes and other wild animals made their dens in the ruins of the gate, and thieves and

* The "Rashōmon" was the largest gate in Kyoto, the ancient capital of Japan. It was 106 feet wide and 26 feet deep, and was topped with a ridge-pole; its stone-wall rose 75 feet high. This gate was constructed in 789 when the then capital of Japan was transferred to Kyoto. With the decline of West Kyoto, the gate fell into bad repair, cracking and crumbling in many places, and became a hideout for thieves and robbers and a place for abandoning unclaimed corpses.

robbers found a home there too. Eventually it became customary to bring unclaimed corpses to this gate and abandon them. After dark it was so ghostly that no one dared approach.

Flocks of crows flew in from somewhere. During the daytime these cawing birds circled round the ridgepole of the gate. When the sky overhead turned red in the afterlight of the departed sun, they looked like so many grains of sesame flung across the gate. But on that day not a crow was to be seen, perhaps because of the lateness of the hour. Here and there the stone steps, beginning to crumble, and with rank grass growing in their crevices, were dotted with the white droppings of crows. The servant, in a worn blue kimono, sat on the seventh and highest step, vacantly watching the rain. His attention was drawn to a large pimple irritating his right cheek.

As has been said, the servant was waiting for a break in the rain. But he had no particular idea of what to do after the rain stopped. Ordinarily, of course, he would have returned to his master's house, but he had been discharged just before. The prosperity of the city of Kyōto had been rapidly declining, and he had been dismissed by his master, whom he had served many years, because of the effects of this decline. Thus, confined by the rain, he was at a loss to know where to go. And the weather had not a little to do with his depressed mood. The rain seemed unlikely to stop. He was lost in thoughts of how to make his living tomorrow, helpless incoherent

thoughts protesting an inexorable fate. Aimlessly
he had been listening to the pattering of the rain on
the Sujaku Avenue.

The rain, enveloping the Rashōmon, gathered
strength and came down with a pelting sound that
could be heard far away. Looking up, he saw a fat
black cloud impale itself on the tips of the tiles jut-
ting out from the roof of the gate.

He had little choice of means, whether fair or
foul, because of his helpless circumstances. If he
chose honest means, he would undoubtedly starve to
death beside the wall or in the Sujaku gutter. He
would be brought to this gate and thrown away like
a stray dog. If he decided to steal...His mind, after
making the same detour time and again, came finally
to the conclusion that he would be a thief.

But doubts returned many times. Though determined that he had no choice, he was still unable to
muster enough courage to justify the conclusion that
he must become a thief.

After a loud fit of sneezing he got up slowly.
The evening chill of Kyōto made him long for the
warmth of a brazier. The wind in the evening dusk
howled through the columns of the gate. The cricket
which had been perched on the crimson-lacquered
column was already gone.

Ducking his neck, he looked around the gate, and
drew up the shoulders of the blue kimono which he
wore over his thin underwear. He decided to spend
the night there, if he could find a secluded corner

sheltered from wind and rain. He found a broad lacquered stairway leading to the tower over the gate. No one would be there, except the dead, if there were any. So, taking care that the sword at his side did not slip out of the scabbard, he set foot on the lowest step of the stairs.

A few seconds later, halfway up the stairs, he saw a movement above. Holding his breath and huddling cat-like in the middle of the broad stairs leading to the tower, he watched and waited. A light coming from the upper part of the tower shone faintly upon his right cheek. It was the cheek with the red, festering pimple visible under his stubbly whiskers. He had expected only dead people inside the tower, but he had only gone up a few steps before he noticed a fire above, about which someone was moving. He saw a dull, yellow, flickering light which made the cobwebs hanging from the ceiling glow in a ghostly way. What sort of person would be making a light in the Rashōmon...and in a storm? The unknown, the evil terrified him.

As quietly as a lizard, the servant crept up to the top of the steep stairs. Crouching on all fours, and stretching his neck as far as possible, he timidly peeped into the tower.

As rumor had said, he found several corpses strewn carelessly about the floor. Since the glow of the light was feeble, he could not count the number. He could only see that some were naked and others clothed. Some of them were women, and all were lolling on the floor with their mouths open or their arms outstretched showing no more signs of life than so many clay dolls. One would doubt that they had ever been alive, so eternally silent they were. Their shoulders, breasts, and torsos stood out in the dim light; other parts vanished in shadow. The offensive smell of these decomposed corpses brought his hand to his nose.

The next moment his hand dropped and he stared. He caught sight of a ghoulish form bent over a corpse. It seemed to be an old woman, gaunt, gray-haired, and nunnish in appearance. With a pine torch in her right hand, she was peeping into the face of a corpse which had long black hair.

Seized more with horror than curiosity, he even forgot to breathe for a time. He felt the hair of his head and body stand on end. As he watched, terrified, she wedged the torch between two floor boards and, laying hands on the head of the corpse, began to pull out the long hairs one by one, as a monkey kills the lice of her young. The hair came out smoothly with the movement of her hands.

As the hair came out, fear faded from his heart, and his hatred toward the old woman mounted. It grew beyond hatred, becoming a consuming antipathy against all evil. At this instant if anyone had brought up the question of whether he would starve to death or become a thief—the question which had occurred to him a little while ago—he would not have hesitated to choose death. His hatred toward evil flared up like the piece of pine wood which the old woman had stuck in the floor.

He did not know why she pulled out the hair of the dead. Accordingly, he did not know whether her case was to be put down as good or bad. But in his eyes, pulling out the hair of the dead in the Rashōmon on this stormy night was an unpardonable crime. Of course it never entered his mind that a little while ago he had thought of becoming a thief.

Then, summoning strength into his legs, he rose from the stairs and strode, hand on sword, right in front of the old creature. The hag turned, terror in her eyes, and sprang up from the floor, trembling. For a small moment she paused, poised there, then lunged for the stairs with a shriek.

"Wretch! Where are you going?" he shouted, barring the way of the trembling hag who tried to scurry past him. Still she attempted to claw her way by. He pushed her back to prevent her...they struggled, fell among the corpses, and grappled there. The issue was never in doubt. In a moment he had her by the arm, twisted it, and forced her down to the floor. Her arms were all skin and bones, and there was no more flesh on them than on the shanks of a chicken. No sooner was she on the floor than he drew his sword and thrust the silver-white blade before her very nose. She was silent. She trembled as if in a fit, and her eyes were open so wide that they were almost out of their sockets, and her breath come in hoarse gasps. The life of this wretch was his now.

This thought cooled his boiling anger and brought a calm pride and satisfaction. He looked down at her, and said in a somewhat calmer voice:

"Look here, I'm not an officer of the High Police Commissioner. I'm a stranger who happened to pass by this gate. I won't bind you or do anything against you, but you must tell me what you're doing up here."

Then the old woman opened her eyes still wider, and gazed at his face intently with the sharp red eyes of a bird of prey. She moved her lips, which were wrinkled into her nose, as though she were chewing something. Her pointed Adam's apple moved in her thin throat. Then a panting sound like the cawing of a crow came from her throat:

"I pull the hair...I pull out the hair...to make a wig."

Her answer banished all unknown from their encounter and brought disappointment. Suddenly she was only a trembling old woman there at his feet. A ghoul no longer: only hag who makes wigs from the hair of the dead—to sell, for scraps of food. A cold contempt seized him. Fear left his heart, and his former hatred entered. These feelings must have been sensed by the other. The old creature, still clutching the hair she had pulled off the corpse, mumbled out these words in her harsh broken voice:

"Indeed, making wigs out of the hair of the dead may seem a great evil to you, but these that are here deserve no better. This woman, whose beautiful black hair I was pulling, used to sell cut and dried snake flesh at the guard barracks, saying that it was dried fish. If she hadn't died of the plague, she'd be selling it now. The guards liked to buy from her, and used to say her fish was tasty. What she did couldn't be wrong, because if she hadn't, she would have starved to death. There was no other choice. If she knew I had to do this in order to live, she probably wouldn't care."

He sheathed his sword, and, with his left hand on its hilt, he listened to her meditatively. His right hand touched the big pimple on his cheek. As he listened, a certain courage was born in his heart—the courage which he had not had when he sat under the gate a little while ago. A strange power was driving him in the opposite direction of the courage which he had had when he seized the old woman. No longer did he wonder whether he should starve to death or become a thief. Starvation was so far from his mind that it was the last thing that would have entered it.

"Are you sure?" he asked in a mocking tone, when she finished talking. He took his right hand from his pimple, and, bending forward, seized her by the neck and said sharply:

"Then it's right if I rob you. I'd starve if I didn't."

He tore her clothes from her body and kicked her roughly down on the corpses as she struggled and tried to clutch his leg. Five steps, and he was at the top of the stairs. The yellow clothes he had wrested off were under his arm, and in a twinkling he had rushed down the steep stairs into the abyss of night. The thunder of his descending steps pounded in the hollow tower, and then it was quiet.

Shortly after that the hag raised up her body from the corpses. Grumbling and groaning, she crawled to the top stair by the still flickering torchlight, and through the gray hair which hung over her face, she peered down to the last stair in the torch light.

Beyond this was only darkness. . . unknowing and unknown.

YAM GRUEL

This story might have taken place about eleven hundred years ago. The exact time does not matter. All that the reader has to know is that the remote past of the Heian period forms its background. In those days there lived in Kyoto a certain samurai in the service of Regent Fujiwara Mototsune. I would specify his name, but unfortunately it is not recorded in the ancient chronicles. Probably he was so ordinary a man as to be unworthy of recording in a chronicle. The writers of these works evidently took very little interest in the lives or stories of common people. In this respect they differ greatly from the present-day writers of the naturalist school. However, the novelists of the Heian period were not as leisurely as might be expected. Anyway, among the samurai in the service of Fujiwara Mototsune there was an official of fifth class court rank. He is the hero of this story. In those days an official of fifth class court rank was a low official. The Japanese word for that rank is "goi." So in this story he will be called "Goi."

Goi was a very plain-looking man. His hollow cheeks made his chin seem unusually long. His lips ...if we mentioned his every striking feature, there would be no end. He was extremely homely and sloppy in appearance.

No one knows how he came to serve the Regent.

Still it is certain that he had gone about his daily chores for a long time, in his discolored silk robe and soft head-gear. From his mannerisms and his unkempt dress, it was hard to believe he had ever been a young man. He was well past forty. His face gave the impression that ever since birth he had had his cold-looking red nose and unshapely mustache exposed to the wind blowing down the Sujaku Avenue. Everyone from the Regent to the herdsmen believed so and had no doubt about it.

You can easily imagine the kind of treatment Goi received from those around him. His fellow samurai did not care a straw for him. His subordinates, with or without court rank, nearly twenty altogether, were also amazingly indifferent to him. When he was supposed to give them instructions, they disregarded him and carried on with their idle chatter and gossip. His existence no more entered their vision than the air itself. His appearance caused no more ripple of unrest than a drop of water in the Japan Sea. The backwash of this man's helplessness was felt in the samurai's hall, where the Steward, the Chief and all his superiors would have nothing to do with him. They gave him all their commands by visual signs.

It is not by accident that man has a voice. Human speech was not made by a simple process. So sometimes they failed to make themselves understood by him. Then they seemed to attribute their failure to defects in his own understanding. Whenever they could not make themselves understood, they would glare at him as if it were his fault. Then, after eyeing him from the top of his head-gear, which was bent out of shape, to the tip of his worn-out straw sandals, they would suddenly turn their backs on him. For all that, Goi never took offence. He was such a timid and unspirited man that he was impervious to all injustice.

His fellow samurai thought it great sport to make him the butt of their jokes. The older men constantly made off-color remarks about his personal appearance; this prompted the younger men to practise all their wit on the helpless Goi. In his presence they would never tire of making critical comments about his nose, mustache, head-gear, and silk robe. Moreover, they would often talk of his hare-lipped wife from whom he had separated five or six years ago, and of a drunken Buddhist priest who was said to have been intimate with his wife. And not only that. Now and again they would play practical jokes on him. It is impossible to enumerate them all. If I mention that once they drank off the rice-wine in his bamboo receptacle and put their waste into it afterwards, you can imagine the kind of tricks they played on him.

But Goi was utterly insensible to this ridicule. At least to the eyes of on lookers he seemed insensible. Whatever others said of him, his expression remained unchanged. Silently stroking his thin mustache, he went on with his daily chores and seemed no more wounded than a duck thrown into a pond. When his comrades went to such extremes as to fix a piece of paper on his top-knot or to tie a straw sandal on his scabbard, he sadly remonstrated, "Why did you do that?" And his expression made you wonder whether he was smiling or crying. Everyone who saw his innocuous face or heard his thin, squeaky voice would feel a momentary compassion and say to himself, "It's not only Goi who's being teased by us. Somebody—many others we don't know are speaking against our stony hearts through his face and voice." But very few of them retained this compassion for any length of time. Among those who felt truly sorry for him was a samurai without rank. He came from the province of Tamba, and was a youth beginning to grow a mustache. Of course, at first he, too, joined the others in ridiculing the red-nosed Goi without reason. But one day he happened to hear Goi's question, "Why did you do that?" and the words stuck in his mind. From that time on he saw Goi in a different light, because he saw a blubberer, persecuted by a hard life, peeping from the pale and stupid face of the undernourished Goi. This samurai could never think of Goi without being impressed by his accusing protest against the hard and heartless realities of life. At the same time Goi's frost-bitten red nose and mustache, the hairs of which might be counted on one's fingers, somehow seemed to give him a touch of consolation.

But this young samurai was an exception. Aside from a few such people, Goi had to continue his

dog's life amid the contempt of everyone around him.
First of all, he had no clothes worthy of the name. He
had only a dark blue coat and a pleated gown of the
same color. But these clothes had faded into what
could be called neither indigo nor blue. As for his
gown, it was exceedingly worn. His thin legs under
this gown, without even drawers, were no more pre-
sentable than the plodding legs of a lean ox pulling
the cart of a poor court-noble. His sword was nondescript, with doubtful metal fittings and with the
lacquer on its hilt beginning to wear off. The red-
nosed Goi used to walk about with short steps, his
round shoulders all the more stooped under a cold
sky, and cast covetous looks right and left. So he
was naturally made a fool of even by passing peddlers. The following instance may be mentioned.

One day on his way from Sanjōmon to Shinsen-en,
he saw several children gathered at the roadside.
Thinking they might be spinning tops, he watched
them, from behind, and found them thrashing a stray,
shaggy dog, held by a rope fastened round his neck.
The shy Goi had almost always been too timid to
translate into action whatever he might have really
felt. But on this occasion, since they were children,
he could muster up some courage.

"Please spare him," he said, smiling as broadly
as possible and patting the shoulder of the boy who
seemed the oldest of the group. "If you hit the dog,
you'll hurt him."

The boy looked back, and turning up his eyes,

stared at him contemptuously. "Mind your own business," he retorted. And, taking a step backward, he pouted his proud lips and shouted, "What? You, red-nosed wretch!"

Goi felt as if these words had struck his face. It was not that he had taken the least offence at the boy's abusive language, but that he felt miserable for having disgraced himself by an unnecessary remark. Concealing his shame with a bitter smile, he silently went on toward Shinsen-en. The children behind made faces and thrust out their tongues at him. Of course he did not see them. Even if he had, it would have made no difference to the spiritless Goi.

Was the hero of this story a man who was born only to be despised, and had he no particular aim in life? No, not so. For the past five or six years he had had an extraordinary craving for yam gruel. Yam gruel is a gruel made by boiling slices of yam in a soup of sweet arrow root. In those days it was regarded as the supreme delicacy, even at the dining table of the sovereign of the realm. Accordingly, such lower officials as Goi could taste it only once a year when they were invited as extraordinary guests to the Regent's Palace. On such an occasion they could eat no more of it than barely enough to moisten their lips. So it had been his long-cherished desire to satiate himself with yam gruel. Of course he did not confide his desire to anyone. He himself might not have been clearly aware that it had been his life-long wish. But as a matter of fact, it would hardly be too much to say that he lived for this purpose. A man sometimes devotes his life to a desire which he is not sure will ever be fulfilled. Those who laugh at this folly are, after all, no more than mere spectators of life.

On January 2nd of a certain year, extraordinary guests were invited to a banquet held in the palace of Fujiwara Mototsune. (This was the banquet held by the Prime Minister Regent inviting State Ministers and other court-nobles, and was much the same as the grand banquet held at the Ninomiya Court on the same day.) Goi and other samurai joined in the dinner; for at that time there was not yet the custom of dividing the guests according to their court ranks, and so all the retainers used to assemble in one hall and enjoy the same feast. At banquets in those old days they served a large assortment of dishes and sweets, few of which would be specially appetizing to moderns: glutinous rice cake, fried and sweetened rice cake, steamed ear-shells, dried fowl, the sweet fish of the Uji River, the crucian of Omi, porgy powdered and seasoned, boiled salmon, broiled octopus, large lobsters, large and small tangerines, mandarins, persimmons dried on skewers, and many others. Among these was the yam gruel in question. Every year Goi looked forward to this yam gruel. But this year, since there were a great many guests, his share of yam gruel was proportionately small.

And, though it may have been only his fancy, it seemed that the yam gruel tasted more delicious than usual. After he had finished it, his eyes were still riveted on the empty bowl. Wiping the drops off his thin mustache, he remarked to someone near by, "I wonder if I shall ever eat my fill of yam gruel."

"He says he hasn't had enough yam gruel," some-one laughed. It was a sonorous and dignified warrior-like voice. Goi, raising his head, looked timidly toward the speaker. The voice came from Fujiwara Toshihito, the son of Tokinaga, who was Finance Minister under the regency of Mototsune. He was a towering and sinewy broad-shouldered giant, and appeared to be well on his way to intoxication, thanks to the many cups of dark-colored rice-wine he had consumed during the meal.

"I'm sorry for you," Toshihito continued, in a voice mingling contempt and compassion, as he saw Goi raise his head. "You shall fill yourself with yam gruel, if you like."

A dog, constantly teased, will not readily jump at a piece of meat thrown to him once in a while. With his usual expression that made you wonder whether he was smiling or crying, Goi looked from Toshihito's face to his empty bowl, contemplating each in turn.

"Don't you care to?" Toshihito asked.

Goi remained silent.

"What would you say?" Toshihito urged.

Goi felt that the eyes of all the company were

focussed on him. Whether he would be the butt of
their ridicule depended on how he would answer.
Whatever he answered, he would be made a fool of,
he thought. So he hesitated. Had the other not just
then thundered impatiently, "If you don't care to, I
won't repeat my invitation," he would have only gone
on comparing Toshihito and his bowl.

"I would be much obliged, sir," Goi answered at
last, when he heard Toshihito's resounding question.

The company listening to this by-play between
Toshihito and Goi roared with laughter. "I would
be much obliged, sir," someone mimicked. Uproari-
ous laughter swept over the group, and the soft and
stiff head-gear of the guests bobbed like waves over
the yellow, blue, crimson, and vari-colored dishes set
before them. Above all, it was Toshihito who laughed
the heartiest.

"Then I'll invite you before long," he choked out.
Apparently the wine had stuck in his throat. "Are
you sure?" he asked emphatically.

"Yes, I would be much obliged, sir" Goi stam-
mered once more, blushing. Of course all the company laughed again. Toshihito himself, who had
asked the question emphatically to make Goi repeat
these very words, laughed still more loudly and
heartily, and his broad shoulders shook as if he were
all the more amused. The rustic court-noble from
the north knows only two ways of getting along in
life: drinking and laughing.

Finally the center of conversation turned else-

where—presumably because the others disliked having their attention concentrated on red-nosed Goi, for
all the amusement of ridiculing him. At any rate,
the topic shifted from one thing to another, and by
the time there was little left to eat and drink, the
company's interest was drawn to the story of a fledg-
ling samurai who tried to get on a horse while he had
both his legs in one side of a pair of riding breeches.
All but Goi listened. He remained aloof, offering no
comment one way or the other. Yam gruel occupied
all his thoughts. He would not even put a cup of
rice-wine to his mouth. Both hands on his lap, as
shy as a girl at an interview with a prospective husband, and blushing even to the roots of his graging
hair, he gazed into his empty black-lacquered cup and
smiled stupidly.

One morning, a few days later, Toshihito invited
Goi to accompany him on a ride to a hot spring near
Higashiyama. Goi, taking him at his word, was only
too glad to accept the offer. Since he had not bathed
for a long time, he had been itching from head to
foot. It would be a godsend if, in addition to being
treated to yam gruel, he could take a bath. So he
got astride the roan that Toshihito had brought.

Soon both Toshihito and Goi were riding toward
Awataguchi down a road along the bank of the Kamo
River. Toshihito, with his black mustache and handsome side-locks, dressed in a dark azure hunting outfit
and armed with a long sword, made a fine picture of
a warrior. Goi, in a shabby, pale silk robe and two

thinly wadded undergarments, his sash tied slovenly around his waist, and the mucus from his nose covering his upper lip, seemed a poor counterpart to the dashing Toshihito. The only comparison was in the horses. Both rode such gallant young steeds—Toshihito on a sorrel and Goi on a roan—that all peddlers and samurai turned to stare at them. Keeping pace with the horses, two servants trotted behind, a valet and a footman.

Although it was winter, it was one of those exceptionally clear mornings. The air was so calm there was not a breath of wind to sway the dead lotus leaves on the slow waters of the river, winding their way through the stones on the white river bed. The leafless branches of low willow trees facing the river were bathed in satin-smooth sunlight, and even the motion of a kingfisher perched on a tree-top cast its distinct shadow on the road. Mt. Hiei showed its whole velvety frost-bitten shoulder over the dark green of Higashiyama. Both Toshihito and Goi made their way leisurely toward Awataguchi, the mother-of-pearl work of their saddles glittering brilliantly in the golden sunlight.

"Where is it that you're pleased to take me, sir?" asked Goi, pulling up the reins.

"Just over there. It's not as far as you might think," Toshihito answered.

"Then is it near Awataguchi?"

"Yes, that will be about it."

When they had ridden abreast as far as Awataguchi, Goi found that this did not appear to be Toshihito's destination. In the course of time they rode past Awataguchi.

"Are we going to stop at Awataguchi?"

"No, a little farther on."

Toshihito rode quietly with a smile, intentionally avoiding Goi's face. The houses on both sides gradually became few and far between, till nothing was visible in the broad paddy fields but crows seeking prey, and in the distance the lingering snow on the northern side of the mountain dimmed into a pale blue. The thorny tops of the unclad trees piercing sharp into the clear sky added to the chill of the air.

"Then, is it about Yamashina, sir?"

"No, this is Yamashina. Our destination is a little farther."

As they jogged on, they rode past Yamashina and much further. They went even beyond Sekiyama, and a little after noon they found themselves in front of the Mie Temple. In this temple lived a priest who was on close terms with Toshihito. They paid a call on the priest, and he served them dinner. After dinner, they rode on hastily. The road farther on was much more lonely than the road they had already covered. In those days the whole country swarmed with robbers, and was unsafe everywhere.

"It's still farther off, isn't it, sir?" Goi asked, looking up into Toshihito's face and hunching his round shoulders all the more.

Toshihito smiled. It was the sort of smile that a

child who has done mischief gives his parent when he has nearly been found out. It seemed as if the wrinkles at the tip of his nose and the slack muscles at the corners of his eyes were deciding whether or not to burst into laughter.

"As a matter of fact, I plan to take you as far as Tsuruga," Toshihito said cheerfully at last, and, raising his whip, he pointed to the distant sky. Under his whip the limpid waters of Lake Biwa shone in the light of the afternoon sun.

"Oh, Tsuruga?" Goi asked in consternation. "The Tsuruga in the Province of Echizen?"

He had often heard that Toshihito had lived in Tsuruga for the most part, since he married the heiress to Fujiwara Arihito, but till that moment he had not had the least idea that Toshihito was going to take him so far. First of all he wondered how, with only two servants, he could ever get safely to distant Echizen across the many mountains and rivers. And then he thought of the frequent rumors that travelers had been killed by robbers. He raised an imploring face to Toshihito.

"Lord bless me!" Goi blubbered out. "First I thought our destination was Higashiyama, but it turned out to be the Mie Temple. Finally you tell me you're going to take me to Tsuruga in Echizen. Whatever do you mean? If you'd told me so at first, I'd have brought my servant with me at least. ... Tsuruga, Lord bless me!"

If his craving for yam gruel had not encouraged

47

him, he would probably have left Toshihito and returned to Kyoto alone.

"Consider one Toshihito a thousand men strong.
You needn't worry about our trip." Toshihito scoffed,
frowning slightly as he saw Goi's consternation. Calling his valet, he slung on the quiver which the valet
had carried on his back and, fastening on his saddle
the black lacquered bow which the valet had carried
in his hand, he rode on at the head of the party. Now
there was no course left for the dispirited Goi but
blind obedience to Toshihito's will. So, helplessly
looking at the desolate wilderness all around, he made
his weary way. The footsteps of his horse were un-
steady; and his own red nose was bent toward the
saddle-bow as he chanted the sutra of the Merciful
Goddess, which he remembered faintly.

The bleak wild fields echoing the rattle of their
horses' hoofs were covered with a vast expanse of
yellow pampas grass, and the cold puddles lying here
and there seemed as if they would freeze that winter
afternoon, with the blue sky mirrored in them. Far
on the horizon, a range of mountains, out of the sun,
lacked even the glitter of the lingering snow, and
painted the horizon with a long streak of dark violet.
But, in places, dreary clumps of dead pampas grass
cut them off from the view of the servants trudging
along.

"Look!" Toshihito called out to Goi suddenly,
turning. "There comes a good messenger. I'll have
him send word to Tsuruga."

Unable to understand what had been said, Goi timidly looked in the direction to which Toshihito had pointed with his bow. Of course there was not another soul in the whole extent of the plain. But in a clump of bushes entangled by a wild vine, a fox could be seen walking slowly, his fur exposed to the declining sunlight. Instantly the fox sprang up hastily and began to run away at full speed. For suddenly Toshihito had whipped up his horse and galloped toward him. Goi also ran for his life, as if in delirium, after Toshihito. Nor could the servants afford to lag behind them. For some time the clatter of their horses' hoofs striking against stones broke the silence of the wilderness. But it was not long until Toshihito stopped his horse, and dangled the fox, which he had caught before the others knew it, head downwards by the side of the saddle. He must have run him down under his horse and caught him alive. Wiping off the drops of perspiration which were clinging to his side-locks, Goi rode pantingly up to Toshihito.

"Now listen, fox!" Toshihito said in a purposely dignified voice, holding the fox high up before his eyes. "Run to Toshihito's mansion in Tsuruga tonight, and tell them *'Toshihito is coming down just now, along with a special guest. Send some men to meet him as far as Takashima about ten o'clock tomorrow morning, and bring two saddled horses.'* Be sure, will you?"

When he finished talking, Toshihito gave the fox a swing and threw him away toward a clump of grass.

"Oh, how he runs! How he runs!" The two servants, who had barely caught up to Toshihito, cheered and clapped their hands as the fox scampered away. The autumn-leaf colored animal was seen running full tilt to the end of the world across stones and over the roots of trees in the evening light. They could see him clearly from the little height where they were standing. For while they had been running after the fox, they had come to the top of an easy slop of the wild fields which merged into the dry river bed.

"He's a messenger of the gods, isn't he, sir?" Giving vent to his naive wonder and admiration, Goi looked up, all the more respectfully, into the face of the fierce knight who commanded the willing service of even a fox. He did not think of what a gulf lay between him and Toshihito. He merely felt with greater assurance that, since he had now fallen more and more under the sway of Toshihito, his own will had become all the freer in the broad embrace of this hero's will. Probably flattery has its natural birth on such an occasion. Therefore, even if the reader should hereafter find the red-nosed Goi something of a sycophant, he should not indiscriminately doubt his character.

The fox, which had been thrown away, rushed down the sloping field as if rolling along, jumped nimbly over the stones in the dry river bed, and ran obliquely up the opposite slope with vigor and agility. Dashing up the incline, the fox looked back and saw the party of samurai that had caught him still abreast on horseback on the far-off top of the easy slope. They all looked as small as fingers standing together. Especially the sorrel and the roan, bathed in the splendor of the setting sun, were in sharp relief against the frosty air.

Turning his head forward, the fox started running again like the wind through the dead pampas grass.

The party arrived at the outskirts of Takashima about ten o'clock the next day, as had been expected. It was a little hamlet facing Lake Biwa, with only a few straw-thatched houses scattered haphazardly in the fields. Threatening clouds filled the sky, unlike the summery sky of yesterday. The rippling surface of the lake mirrored the dappled picture of pine trees growing on its bank. Presently the travelers stopped. Toshihito turned to Goi and said, "Look! Over there some men are coming to meet us."

Of the twenty or thirty men who were bringing two saddled horses, some were on horseback and others were on foot. Their silk robes fluttering in the cold wind, they all came rapidly toward them along the bank of the lake and through the pine-trees. As soon as they neared Toshihito, the mounted men hurriedly jumped down out of their saddles, while those on foot kneeled down on the ground, and they all waited respectfully for Toshihito.

"Indeed, the fox seems to have done a messenger's

service," said Goi.

"Yes," Toshihito replied, "the fox is an animal that has a natural ability to disguise itself. So it's quite easy for it to perform such a service."

While Goi and Toshihito were talking in this vein, they and their party came to where Toshihito's vassals were waiting.

"Thank you for coming," Toshihito called out to them. The vassals, who had all been kneeling on the ground, stood up at once and bridled the horses of Toshihito and Goi.

The two had scarecely got off and sat down on fur cushions when a gray-haired vassal in a brown silk robe came before Toshihito and said, "Last evening a mysterious thing took place."

"Well, what was it?" Toshihito asked in a lordly manner, offering Goi the food and drink which his vassals had brought.

"Please, my lord. Last evening about eight o'clock Her Ladyship fell unconscious and said, '*I am the fox of Sakamoto. I will give you a message my lord has sent today. So step up to me and listen.* All of us got together before her. Then she said, '*My husband is coming just now with a special guest. Around ten o'clock tomorrow morning send men as far as the outskirts of Takashima and take two saddled horses.*' That was the message she gave us."

"That's very mysterious," Goi chimed in importantly, with a remark, pleasing to everyone.

"Her Ladyship told us in no ordinary way," the

vassal went on. "Trembling with terror, she said, *'Don't be late. If you are late, I will be punished by my husband.'* While talking, she wept incessantly.

"What did she do after that?"

"After that she fell asleep. When we left, she seemed to be still asleep."

"What do you say?" Toshihito asked, turning his proud look to Goi when his vassal had finished talking. "Even animals serve Toshihito."

Bobbing his head and scratching his big red nose, Goi answered theatrically, "I'm filled with admiration beyond words." He then rolled his tongue over his upper lip to lap up the drops of the rice wine left on his mustache.

It was the same evening. Goi was passing a long sleepless night in a room in Toshihito's mansion, his eyes casually fixed on a rush light.

Then the picture of the pine-grown hills, the brooks, withered fields, grass, leaves, stones, and the smell of the smoke of field fires—all these things, one after another, passed through his mind. The pleasant relief he had felt on seeing the red glow of the charcoal in the long brazier when they had arrival earlier that evening—it, too, could only be considered an event of the distant past.

Stretching his legs out under the luxurious yellow ceremonial robe, which Toshihito had lent him, Goi tried to patch together the events of the evening. His liquor-filled brain made it almost impossible. Beneath the ceremonial robe, he was wearing two thickly wadded garments of a russet color, which Toshihito had also lent him. Under this comfortable warmth Goi realized that now he lay in the lap of wealth. The night was bitter cold, he imagined. The meager events of his life compared to the ones he had experienced tonight seemed like those of a coolie compared to a prince. But for all that, there was a curious uneasiness in his mind. Above all, he was impatient for time to pass. Yet, on the other hand, somehow he felt that dawn, that is, the eating of yam gruel, must not come too soon. Nervousness from this sudden change in circumstance lurked at the back of his mind, chilling his heart and keeping him awake.

By and by he heard someone shouting in the large yard outside. To judge from the voice, it was the gray-haired vassal who had come part of the way to meet Toshihito. It sounded as if he were making some kind of special announcement.

"Listen, all you servants. His Lordship wants each of you, young and old, to bring a yam three inches wide and five feet long, by six o'clock in the morning. Remember, by six o'clock." The old man's dry voice resounded through the frosty air, and his very words seemed to penetrate to the marrow of Goi's bones. Unconsciously, he drew his ceremonial robe tight around him.

The command was repeated. Then human noises

ended, and all was again hushed into the dead silence of the winter night. The servants had gone to obey the order—probably in fear of their lives, Goi imagined. Alone with his thoughts once more, he tossed and turned. Finally he lay still. An oppressive silence filled the room, broken only by the sizzling oil in the rush lamp. The red light of the wick was wavering.

So after all he was to have yam gruel. When he thought of this, the old uneasiness which had left him because of the distraction of what was happening outside, came back again. His perverse reluctance to being treated to yam gruel too soon grew stronger than ever, and it continued to dominate his thoughts. Such an early realization of his heart's desire seemed to turn years of patient waiting into a vain endeavor. If possible, he wished that something unexpected would happen to keep him from eating yam gruel for a while. Such ideas spun round and round in his mind like a top. At last, overcome by fatigue from his long journey, he fell fast asleep.

The next morning when he wakened, the thought of yam gruel was on his mind. He must have overslept. It was past six o'clock. He jumped out of bed, crossed the floor, and opened the window. Outside he saw stacked roof high what at first glance appeared to be huge piles of corded logs. Rubbing his sleepy eyes, he looked a second time, and with a sharp gasp he realized what they were. Yams! Yams! Yams! Tremendously large yams three inches wide and five feet long, enough to feed the whole town of Tsuruga. Set out in the broad yard, five or six caldrons were placed side by side on new spikes driven into the ground, and dozens of young maids in white-lined garments worked as busily as bees around them. Some of the servant girls were lighting fires, some were raking ashes, and others were pouring sweet-arrow root juice into the caldrons from wooden pails. Volumes of smoke rose from under the caldrons, and bursts of white vapor shot up from them to mix with the still lingering haze of dawn and form a gray pall which hung all over the large yard, obscuring every-thing but the red flames of the blazing fires. The wide yard was in such a state of confused excitement as is witnessed only on a battlefield or at the scene of a fire. These huge caldrons boiling yams into gruel filled Goi with blank amazement and dismay. They made him remember only too clearly that he had made the long journey to Tsuruga all the way from Kyoto for the express purpose of eating yam gruel. The more he thought, the more miserable he felt about everything. By this time he had already lost half of the appetite which had hitherto commanded our sympathy for him.

An hour later he sat at breakfast with Toshihito and his father-in-law, Arihito. In front of him was a huge vat filled to the brim with a tremendous sea of yam gruel. Earlier he had seen dozens of spirited young men deftly wield kitchen knives to slice up that pile of yams which reached high up to the eaves of the house. He had seen the maids run here and there past one another, scooping all the yam slices into the caldrons. When all the yams piled up on the large mats were gone, he had seen clouds of steam, reeking with the smell of yams and arrow-root, rise from the caldrons into the clear morning air. Naturally enough, when Goi, who had watched these things, was served yam gruel in a huge pitcher, he felt satiated even before tasting the delicacy. Sitting in front of the pitcher, he wiped his perspiring brow in embarrassment.

"I hear you haven't had your fill of yam gruel," said Arihito's father-in-law, "please help help yourself without reserve." And he ordered the servant boys to bring several more large pitchers of yam gruel. Goi put about half of the yam gruel from the pitcher into a big earthen vessel, and closing his eyes, he reluctantly drank it off, his red nose becoming all the redder.

"As my father said, you needn't be hesitant," grinning maliciously, Toshihito also pressed Goi to have another pitcherful of yam gruel. Goi was in a terrible plight. Frankly, he had not wanted to eat even one bowful of yam gruel even at the beginning. With great endurance he managed to do justice to half a pitcherful of it. If he took any more, he thought he would throw it up before swallowing it. But to refuse to eat any more would be to spurn the kindness of Toshihito and Arihito. So closing his eyes again, he drained off a third of the remaining half.

He could not take another mouthful.

"I'm more than obliged to you," Goi mumbled incoherent thanks. He was in such pitiful embarrassment that drops of perspiration formed on his mustache and the tip of his nose, as if it were midsummer instead of winter.

"How sparingly you eat!" said Arihito. "Our guest seems to be reserved. Boys, don't be idle." At his words, the servants tried to pour more yam gruel from the new pitchers into the earthen vessel. Waving both his hands, as if to drive off flies, Goi expressed his earnest desire to be excused.

If at this time Toshihito had not unexpected said, "Look over there," pointing to the eaves of the house opposite, Arihito would still have continued to press the yam gruel on Goi. But fortunately Toshihito's voice drew everyone's attention toward the eaves. The morning sun was shedding its light on the cypress-shingle roof. An animal sat quietly on the eaves, its sleek fur bathed in the bright sunshine. It was the fox of Sakamoto which Toshihito had caught with his hands in the withered fields two days before.

"The fox has also come from a desire for yam gruel. Men, give him his feed." Toshihito's orders were promptly executed. The fox jumped down from the eaves and immediately began to feast on yam gruel.

Watching the fox eat its meal, Goi looked back with fond longing on his past life before the time he had come to Tsuruga. What he remembered was that he had been made a fool of by many warriors, and reviled even by Kyoto boys with "What? You Red Nose!" and that he was a pitiful, lonely being, with faded silk robe and nondescript sword, who wandered about Sujaku Avenue like a homeless mongrel. But at the same time he had been happy, treasuring up his desire to gorge himself on yam gruel. With the reassurance that he need not eat any more of it, he felt the perspiration all over his face dry up gradually, beginning at the tip of his nose. The early morning in Tsuruga was fine but cold, and a biting wind was blowing. Hastily grasping his nose, Goi emitted a loud sneeze toward the silver pitcher.

THE MARTYR

Even if one liveth to be three hundred years of age in excess of pleasure, it is but as a dream compared with everlasting pleasure.—*Guide do Pecador*.

He who walketh the path of goodness shall enjoy the mysterious sweetness which pervadeth the doctrine.
—*Imitatione Christi*.

One Christman night some years ago a young Japanese boy was found exhausted and starving at the entrance to the Church of Santa Lucia in Nagasaki. He was taken in and cared for by the Jesuit brothers who were coming into the church. He was given the name Lorenzo, and was thereafter brought up in the church under the wing of the Jesuit missionaries.

When the brothers asked him about his birth and parents, he never revealed his history, but gave such evasive answers as,, "My home is paradise," and "My father is the Father of all." His disarming smile dispelled further questioning as to his past.

It was, however, evident from the blue rosary on his wrist that his family had not been heathens. Perhaps that was the reason why the kindly fathers and brothers took Lorenzo to their heart.

The elders were so struck by this young boy's piety that they came to think of him in time as the incarnation of a cherub, and to love him dearly, though they knew nothing of his past. Moreover, the perfection and purity of his face and form, and his sweet feminine voice made him the darling of everyone.

Of all the brothers, Simeon in particular loved him as if he were his own brother, and in entering and leaving the church they were seen hand in hand. Simeon, born in a military family, once served a certain feudal lord. He was a towering giant with Herculean strength and had more than once defended the Fathers against being stoned by heathens. His harmonious friendship with Lorenzo might have been compared to a fierce eagle taking loving care of a dove or a blooming vine twining around a cedar on Mt. Lebanon.

Meanwhile three years flew by, and the time came for Lorenzo to celebrate his coming to manhood. About this time the rumor spread that Lorenzo and the daughter of an umbrella-maker who lived not far from the Church of Santa Lucia were becoming intimate. Since the umbrella-maker was also a believer in the teachings of the Lord, it was customary for him to come to church with his daughter. Even during the time of prayers this girl never took her eyes from Lorenzo. Still more, in entering and leaving the church she was sure to turn her beautiful and loving eyes toward him. This naturally attracted the notice of the congregation, and some said that she had intentionally stepped on his foot, while others said that they had been seen exchanging love letters.

Since the gossip about the boy and girl had gotten

61

quite out of hand, the Father Superior of the church decided it was time to question his young charge. One day he called Lorenzo to his side. "Lorenzo," he asked gently, stroking his long gray hair, "I have heard unsavory rumors about you and the umbrella-maker's daughter. But surely they can't be true, can they?" Lorenzo, shaking his head sadly, only repeated in a tearful voice, "No, they're not true. They are quite unfounded." After the boy's many tearful denials, the Father, considering his age and constant piety, was finally convinced that Lorenzo was speaking the truth, and dismissed him with a word about good behavior.

Yes, the Father's suspicion was dispelled. But the rumors persisted among the people of Santa Lucia. This scandal particularly worried Lorenzo's dear friend Simeon. At first he was too ashamed to make a searching inquiry into such a licentious affairs, and he was unable not only to ask Lorenzo but even to look him in the eye.

However, once he happened to pick up in the back garden of Santa Lucia, a love letter from the girl addressed to Lorenzo. Thrusting it into Lorenzo's face, and threatening and coaxing, Simeon questioned him in many ways. But Lorenzo, his handsome face blushing, merely said, "I hear the girl has given her heart to me, but I only received letters from her, and I have never even talked with her." Simeon, who felt the weight of the town's opinion, pressed further questions on his brother. Lorenzo, gazing at the other with his sad, reproachful look, said, "Do I look like a liar even to you?" and left the room like a swallow leaving his nest. At these words, Simeon felt a great shame come over him for having been suspicious of his brother and was leaving, with his head bowed, when suddenly the boy Lorenzo rushed in, threw his arms around Simeon's neck, and panted out in a whisper, "I was wrong. Forgive me." Before Simeon could answer a word, he rushed out the way he had come, hurrying as if to conceal his tear-stained face. Simeon did not know whether Lorenzo felt guilty for his intimacy with the girl or for his rude behavior.

Sometime later the people of the town were shocked at the news that the umbrella-maker's daughter was soon to become a mother. She told her father that the child in her womb was that of Lorenzo. The old umbrella-maker in great rage immediately carried the accusation to the priests of Santa Lucia. Lorenzo, who was summoned before them, said "It's not so," but could make no excuse to justify himself against such evidence. The same day the fathers and all the brothers sat in conference and sentenced Lorenzo to excommunication. His excommunication, that is, his banishment from the church, would immediately deprive him of the means of livelihood. But it would invite disgrace on the glory of the Lord and the congregation to keep the sinner in Santa Lucia. Therefore, the brothers who held him dear are said to have driven him away with tears in their eyes.

The most pitiable of all was Simeon, who had been Lorenzo's dearest friend. More vexed by being deceived than grieved at his being driven away, Simeon struck Lorenzo full in his handsome face as he went sadly out of the doorway into the cold winter blast. Knocked off balance by the blow, Lorenzo fell down. But he got up slowly, and looking up to the sky with tearful eyes, he prayed in a quivering voice: "Lord forgive Simeon, for he knows not what he does." Disheartened by these words, Simeon only went on slashing and flailing his arms for a time at the doorway. Finally restrained by the other brothers, he folded his arms, and with his face as fierce as the threatening sky, he glared resentfully at the back of Lorenzo who was sorrowfully leaving the gate of Santa Lucia. According to the story from the brothers who happened to be there, at that very moment Phoebus, quivering in the wintry blast, was driving his crimson orb of day below the western sky of Nagasaki, and the angel of a crestfallen Lorenzo prodding his weary way straight into the light of the heavenly disk seemed to have a nimbus of celestial flame.

After that, Lorenzo was a being changed from the time when he used to offer incense in the chancel of Santa Lucia. He was reduced to wretched beggary and lived in an outcasts' hovel on the edge of the town. Since he was formerly a believer in the Lord's doctrine, he was despised and abused by the heathen rabble, and he could never walk on the streets without being mocked by heartless boys. Time and again he was caned, stoned, or cut at with a sword. Once he lay in the grip of a dreadful fever that raged in the town of Nagasaki; in pain and agony, he writhed by the roadside for seven nights and days. And the God of infinite love and boundless mercy not only rescued him from death, but gave him mountain berries, fish, and shellfish when he was given no alms of money or rice. Thus, morning and evening he prayed as he had in the days at Santa Lucia, and he never took the beads of jasper off his wrist. Moreover, in the dead of night he used to steal out of his outcasts' hovel and in the moonlight make his way as near to Santa Lucia as he dared, to pray for the blessings of Jesus Christ.

The Christians who worshipped at the church paid no heed to the boy, and finally no one, not even the Fathers, felt pity for the boy. Since they were convinced of the truth of the scandalous rumors which prevailed at the time of his excommunication, nothing was farther from their thoughts than that he should ever be a boy of such piety as to make a nightly visit to Santa Lucia alone. This was a great pity for Lorenzo; inevitable as it was, being one of the unfathomable mysteries of God.

In the meantime the old umbrella-maker's daughter gave premature birth to a baby girl, who became a favorite of the stiff-necked old man because she was his first grandchild. He took great care not only of his daughter but also his of grandchild, caressing it in his arms and giving it a doll to play with. This was natural for a grandfather. But Simeon, the brother, was remarkable for his singular conduct. After the girl gave birth to the baby, this young man who looked like a giant strong enough to overpower the devil, called upon the umbrella-maker's family whenever he had spare time, and taking up the infant in his rough arms with tears on his bitter face, he would recall the quiet, ashy and handsome Lorenzo whom he had loved as his younger brother. However, the girl appeared to be grieved and chagrined that Lorenzo, since his excommunication, had not come to see her or her child, and she did not seem pleased that Simeon should call.

Time and tide wait for no man. A year passed like a snowflake that falls into the river, a moment white and then gone forever. Then unexpectedly, a disasterous fire broke out and threatened to ravage all of Nagasaki in one night. Such was the fury of the fire that it appeared as if the trumpet of the last judgment had sounded, rending the flames of the holocaust. Since the umbrella-maker's house was downwind from the fire, it was enveloped in flames in an instant. Terror-stricken, all the family scurried away from the flames, when they suddenly realized that they had left their baby sleeping in another room. All the old man could do was to rave and stamp on the ground. The girl would have rushed back into the burning building to save her baby, had she not been prevented by others. The fierce wind added to its strength every moment, and the pillars of flames soared and raged as if to scorch even the stars in the sky. The townspeople who had banded together to bring the fire under control could do nothing but warn others of the danger, while all that the people who stood by could do was to calm the frenzied girl. At that moment there came Simeon, the brother, pushing his way as easily as if walking through tall grass, since he was a sturdy hero who had felt the sting of bullets and arrows in battles for feudal lords. Quickly grasping the situation, he rushed boldly into the flames but only to flinch before the terrible force of the fire. He had hardly crept into a few clouds of smoke when he beat a hasty retreat. Reappearing before the old man and his daughter, he gasped, "This is the will of God, you must resign yourselves to the inevitable." At that moment "Lord save us!" someone cried by the side of the old man. Since the voice sounded familiar to him, Simeon looked round to see where it came from. It was Lorenzo beyond all doubt. A glance showed the old samurai his angelic face and figure, dressed in rags as he was, his pure, thin face shining in firelight, with his black hair, which, ruffled by the wind, reached down below his shoulders. Poor Lorenzo in the form of a beggar was staring into the blazing house. But that was only for the twinkling of an eye. Scarcely had a terrible wind swept past to fan up the raging flames when he plunged headlong into the pillars of fire, the beams of fire, and the walls of fire. "Lord save us!" cried Simeon, breaking into a cold sweat all over his body, and crossed himself. Somehow at that moment in his mind's eye, he saw the graceful and sorrowful figure of Lorenzo going out of Santa Lucia straight into the light of the heavenly disk quivering in the wintry blast.

The brothers, who were near by, were amazed at Lorenzo's heroic action, but remembered his old offense. At once unsavory comments, on the wings of the wind, swept over the crowd of people. One person and another heaped abuse on him, saying, "Indeed a father is a father. Lorenzo, who hasn't dared come near because of shame for his sin, has just rushed into the fire to save his own child." The old man seemed to agree with their views, and apparently to conceal the agitation of his heart, he was yelling silly things in restless anxiety. Frantically the daughter was down on her knees, covering her face with both hands. She knelt motionless in a trance, offering fervent prayers with all her heart and soul. Sparks of fire fell like rain from the sky. Smoke bellowed over the ground and smote her face. But she was lost in her prayers, forgetting herself and the world around her.

After a time there was a sudden stir among the people crowding before the blazing fire, when Lorenzo with disheveled hair appeared enshrouded in a tower of flames, holding the infant aloft in both arms, as if descending from heaven. One of the beams must have broken then, for with a terrific crash, a volume of smoky flame rose high up into the sky, and the figure of Lorenzo disappeared. And nothing was to be seen but a pillar of blazing fire shooting high up like coral.

Struck by the great misfortune, Simeon, the old man and all the other brothers were stunned and dazed. The girl gave a shriek, and jumped up with her legs exposed, but again prostrated herself on the ground, as if struck by lightning. Be that as it may, before they knew it, the baby girl was found tightly wrapped in the hands of the girl who had thrown herself to the ground. Oh, the boundless and infinite wisdom of God! Words are inadequate to sing the praise of his power. The infant whom Lorenzo had thrown with his last desperate strength as he was struck by the fall of the burning beam, fortunately dropped unhurt at the feet of the mother.

Then there arose from the mouth of the old man a solemn voice in praise of the love of God, together with the voice of the girl who was on the ground weeping tears of joy. In the meantime, Simeon, in his whole-hearted desire to save Lorenzo, had dashed straight into the storm of the raging fire, and the old man's voice rose up into the night sky in an anxious and pathetic prayer. Not only the baby's grandfather but all the Christians standing around the mother and child offered tearful prayers. The son of the Virgin Mary, our Lord Jesus Christ, who regards the sufferings of all men as his own, granted their prayers at last. Behold, Lorenzo, horribly burned, rescued and in Simeon's arms away from the flames and smoke.

Those were not all the misadventures of that night. Lorenzo, gasping for breath, was immediately carried in the arms of the brothers up the hill to Santa Lucia, and was laid at its gate. The umbrella-maker's daughter, choked with tears, had been pressing her baby to her breast, now threw herself on her knees at the feet of the Father Superior and made an unexpected confession of her love affair: "This baby girl is not a child by Lorenzo. To tell you the truth, this is a child I had by becoming intimate with the son of the heathen family next-door." The trembling of the distracted girl's voice and the glistening of her eyes bathed in tears proved beyond all doubt that there was not a shadow of falsehood in her confession. Her startling confession took the breath and voice out of the mouths of the brothers who stood by, hardly aware of the raging and crackling sky-scorching flames.

Wiping away her tears, she continued, "He had such a firm faith in God and treated me so coldly that I came to bear a grudge against him. By making a false statement that the baby was his child, I hoped to have revenge on him for his coldness. But he was too noble-minded to hate me for my sin, and at the risk of his own life, he graciously rescued my baby from the fiery inferno. His love and deeds make me adore him as a Jesus Christ reborn. When I think of my heinous sin, I wouldn't care if my body were torn to pieces by the devil's talons." She had scarcely finished the confession of her love affair before she threw herself to the ground in tears.

At that time the outcries, "Martyr," "Martyr!" surged up from among the Christians who crowded around two and three deep. "Out of his love for the sinner," the voices cried, "he degraded himself to beggary, following in the footsteps of our Lord Jesus Christ. But no man, not even the Father Superior whom he looked up to as his father and Simeon whom he relied on as his brother, knew his heart. What is this but a martyr?"

While listening to the daughter's confession of her love affair, Lorenzo could only nod slightly. His hair was burned, his skin was scorched. He could move neither his hands nor his feet, and now he had no strength left to speak. The old umbrella-maker and Simeon, whose hearts were torn by the girl's confession, ministered to him as best they could on their knees at his side, and bathed his burns in tears. But Lorenzo's breathing became shorter and fainter every minute, and the end was not far off. All that remained unchanged in him now was the color of his star-like eyes looking far up into the sky.

The Father Superior, who had been listening to the girl's confession, with his gray hair waving in the night's windstorm, and with his back turned toward the gate of Santa Lucia, declared to her solemnly, "Blessed are they that repent. How could the human hand ever punish those so blessed? From now on you must observe God's commandments all the better

and await the judgment day." And then, "Lorenzo,"
he said, "your aspiration to emulate our Lord Jesus
Christ in your conduct is a virtue unrivaled among
the Christians in this country. Especially as you are
so young,..." What could the matter be? The
Father, who had gone thus far, suddenly closed his
mouth, and watched Lorenzo as intently as if he had
seen the light of heaven. How reverent he looked!
The shaking of his hands was so extraordinary. The
tears would not stop flowing from the Father's
shriveled cheeks. Suddenly the umbrella-maker and
Simeon stared. The eyes of all followed theirs to two
soft, pure breasts, which stood out among the rags
on the chest of the angel, now lying silently at the
gate of Santa Lucia, bathed in the light of the fire
red as the blood of Jesus Christ at his crucifixion.
Now on Lorenzo's sorely burned face, its natural
gentleness and beauty could no longer be concealed.
It may have been only a moment—it seemed like an
eternity—before the entire assembly realized that
Lorenzo was not a boy but a girl. Yes, Lorenzo was
a girl! Lorenzo was a girl! Behold! With the flames
raging at their back, the brethren circled around
Lorenzo, stood in awe and wonder with their eyes
fastened on the martyr. Lorenzo, driven out of Santa
Lucia on the false charge of adultery, was a fair girl
of this country like the umbrella-maker's daughter
herself.

That moment is said to have inspired them with
as much holy awe as if God's voice had been heard

from far beyond the starry vault of heaven. The Christians who had been standing before Santa Lucia, each and all hung their heads like the heads of wheat blown by the wind, and knelt around Lorenzo. All that was heard was the roar of the flames blazing up into the star-lit sky and the sobbing of people near-by. The sobbing may have come from the umbrella-maker's daughter or from Simeon who had been as good a friend to him as if he were his real brother. Soon the silence was broken by the sad, solemn chant-ing of the scriptures by the reverend Father, his hand raised aloft. When his chanting ceased, "Lorenzo," he called, and the fair-eyed girl quietly breathed her last, with a faint, peaceful smile on her lips, looking up into the glory of Heaven far beyond the dark night.

Nothing else is known of the life of this girl. Yet what does it matter? For the sublimity of life cul-minates in the most precious moment of inspiration. Man will make his life worth living, if he tosses a wave aloft high up into the starry sky, o'er life's dark main of worldy cares, to mirror in its crystal foam the light of the moon yet to rise. Therefore, are not those who know the last of Lorenzo those who know the whole of her life?

POSTSCRIPT

I have in my collection a book entitled 'Legenda Aurea' which was published by the Nagasaki Church. It does not, however, contain only golden legends of

Western Europe. It includes not only the words and deeds of European saints but also the religious devotions of Japanese Christians, presumably to serve evangelical purposes.

This book consists of two volumes, Parts I and II printed on '*mino*' paper (a kind of tough Japanese paper) in '*hiragana*' (the cursive form of the Japanese syllabary) mixed with Chinese characters in cursive style. The lettering is so indistinct that it makes us wonder whether it was printed or not. On the title-page of Volume I, the Latin title is written crosswise, and under the title are written two vertical Chinese lines, "Printed at the beginning of March, the year of Grace 1596." At either side of the date is a picture of an angel blowing a trumpet. It is technically very crude but has a charm of its own. The title-page of Volume II is identical with that of Volume I except for the words, "Printed in the middle of March."

Both volumes contain about sixty pages. Volume I carries its golden legends in eight chapters, and Volume II in ten chapters. Each volume opens with a preface by an unknown writer and a table of contents intermixed with Latin words.

To the Japanese scholar the writing of the preface leaves something to be desired. Here and there we find such intermixtures of literal translation of European writing which makes us wonder if it was not written by a Jesuit priest.

THE MARTYR

'*The Martyr*', here introduced, was taken from Volume II of '*the Legenda Aurea.*' This story is presumably a truthful record of a happening which took place in a Christian church at Nagasaki in those days. However, the actuality of the great fire as recorded in this story is impossible to ascertain even by referring to '*the Nagasaki Minatogusa*' (Miscellanies of the Port of Nagasaki) and other books. Much less is it possible to ascertain the exact date of the occurence.

For publication, I ventured to add some literary embellishment to '*The Martyr.*' I hope that the simple and refined style of the original has not been impaired.

(August, 1919.)

KESA AND MORITO

Looking at the moon in a pensive mood, Morito walks on the fallen leaves outside the fence of his house :

The moon is rising now. I usually wait for moonrise impatiently. But tonight the bright moonrise shocks me with horror. I shudder to think that tonight will destroy my present self and turn me into a wretched murderer. Imagine when these hands will have turned crimson with blood! What a cursed being I shall seem to myself then! My heart would not be so wrung with pain if I were to kill an enemy I hate, but tonight I have to kill a man whom I do not hate.

I have known him a long time. Though it is only lately that I have learned his name, Wataru Saemonno-jo, I have known his handsome face ever since I can remember. When I found that he was Kesa's husband, it is true that I burned with jealousy for a while. But now my jealousy has already faded, leaving no trace in my mind or heart. So for my rival in love, I have neither hatred nor spite. Rather, I think kindly of him. When my aunt, Koromogawa, told me how he spared no pain or effort to win Kesa's heart, I felt sympathetic toward him. I understood that out of his whole-hearted desire to win her for his wife, he even took the trouble to learn to write poetry. I cannot imagine that simple and prosaic man writing love poems, and a smile comes to my lips in spite of myself. This is not a smile of scorn; I am touched by the tenderness of a man who goes to such extremes to win a woman. It is even possible that his passionate love which makes him idolize my beloved Kesa gives me some satisfaction.

But do I really love Kesa? Our love affair may be separated into two stages, the past and the present. I loved her before she married Wataru, or I thought I did. But now that I look into my heart, I find there were many motives. What did I want from her? She was the kind of woman for whom I felt fleshly desire even in the days when I was chaste. If an overstatement is allowed, my love toward her was nothing more than a sentimental embellishment of the motive that drove Adam to Eve. This is evident from my doubts about my continuing to love her if my desire had been fulfilled. Though I kept her in my mind for the three years after the break in our association, I can not surely say I love her. In my later attachment to her, my greatest regret was that I had not known her intimately. Tortured with discontent, I fell into the present relationship, which terrified me, and yet which I knew must come. Now I ask myself anew, "Do I really love her?"

When I met her again after three years at the celebration of the completion of the Watanabe Bridge,

I resorted to all sorts of means to get a chance to meet her secretly. Finally I succeeded. Not only did I succeed in meeting her, but I took her body just as I had been dreaming of. At that time the regret that I had not known her physically was not all that obsessed me. When I sat close to her in the matted room of Koromogawa's house, I noticed that much of my regret had already faded. Probably my desire was weakened by the fact that I was not chaste. But the basic cause was that she was not what I expected her to be. When I sat face to face with her, I found that she was not the image of statuesque beauty, I had imagined for the past three years. She was far from the idol I had idealized in my heart. Her face, thickly coated with leaden powder, has lost much of its bloom and smooth charm. Darkish rings had formed beneath her eyes. What remained unchanged in her was her clear, full, dark eyes. When I saw her in this new light, I was shocked, and in spite of myself I could not help turning my eyes away.

Then how is it that I had intercourse with a woman to whom I felt so little attachment? First I was moved by a strange wish to conquer my former heart's desire. Sitting face to face, she gave me a deliberately exaggerated story of her love for her husband. It left nothing but an empty ringing in my ears. "She has a vainglorious idea of her husband," I thought. I also suspected this may be motivated by her wish not to inflame my desire. At the same time my desire to expose her falsehood worked more and more strongly upon me. Why did I consider it a false-hoods If you tell me, dear reader, that my own con-ceit had led me to suspect the falsehood of her state-ment, I cannot deny your charge. Nevertheless, then I believed and still now do I believe that it was a lie.

But the desire to conquer was not all that obsessed me at that moment. I blush to mention it—I was dominated by lust. It was not merely my regret that I had not known her body. It was a base lust for lust's sake which did not require that the other party be that woman. Probably no man who hired a woman in a brothel would have been baser than I was then.

Anyway, out of such various motives, I had rela-tions with Kesa. Or, rather, I dishonored her. To return to the first question that I put forth, I need not ask myself now if I loved her. When it was over, I raised her up forcibly in my arms—this woman who had thrown herself down crying. Then she look-ed more ignominious than I. Her ruffled hair and sweating flesh, everything indicated the ugliness of her mind and body. It would not be wrong to say that I have had a new hatred for her in my heart since that day. And tonight I am going to murder a man I do not hate, for the sake of a woman I do not love.

"Let's kill Wataru," I whipered into her ear. Mad indeed I must have been to have made such a brazen proposal. Distractedly I breathed into her ear my past desire to challenge Wataru to a fight and win her love. Anyway, "Let's kill Wataru," I whispered, and very surely did I whisper clenching my teeth, in spite of myself. Looking back now, I cannot tell what prompted me to do such a rash thing. All I can think of to explain it is that I wanted to patch up the affair for the present, and that the more I despised and hated her, the more impatient I became to bring some disgrace upon her. Nothing could be more suitable for these purposes than to kill the husband she professed to love, and to wring her consent from her willy-nilly. So, like a man in a nightmare, I must have prevailed upon her to commit between ourselves the murder which I do not wish. If that does not suffice to explain my motive for proposing to murder Wataru, no other explanation can be attempted, except that a power unknown to mortals (maybe a devil or demon) led me into an evil course. Persistently and repeatedly I whispered the same thing into her ear.

Finally she raised her face and said, "Yes, you must kill Wataru." Not only was her ready consent a surprise to me, but I saw a mysterious sparkle in her eye which I had not noticed before. An adulteress —that was the impression she gave me then. Instantly disappointment and horror—and yes, contempt—flashed through my feverish brain. I would have canceled by promise on the spot if it had been possible. Then I could have branded her an adulteres, and my conscience could have taken refuge in righteous indignation. But I was unable to do so. I confess that I readily saw its utter impossibility the moment she suddenly gazed at me. Her attitude changed, as though she had seen through my heart. I fell into the sad plight of making an appointment to murder her husband because of my fear that she would take revenge on me if I failed to carry out my part of the bargain. Now this fear has a firm and persistent vise-like grip on me. Laugh, if you wish, at my cowardice. This is the action of one who did not know how base his paramour could be. "If I don't kill her husband, she will kill me one way or another. I must kill him else she will kill me." I thought desperately, looking into her tearless but crying eyes. After I made the vow, did I not detect a smile on her mouth and a dimple forming on her pale cheek? Oh, because of this cursed pledge, I am going to add the crime of a heinous murder to the blackest heart imaginable. If I were to break this impending appointment which is to be fulfilled tonight,...No, my vow forbids it. This is more than I can bear. For another thing, I am afraid of her revenge. This is quite true. But there is something else that prompts me to the action. What is this? What is that great power which impels me, this coward 'me', to murder an innocent man? I cannot tell. I cannot tell. But possibly. ...No, it cannot be. I despise her. I fear her. I hate her. And yet, and yet, it may be because I love her.

Morito, continuing to pace, says no more. The singing of a ballad comes out of the night.

The human mind is in the dark.
With not a light to shine upon.

It burns a fire of worldly cares
To go and fade in but a span.

PART II. KESA'S MONOLOGUE

*At night under a lamp, Kesa, lost in thought,
biting her sleeve, stands with her back toward the
light :*

Is he coming or isn't he, I wonder. It's highly
unlikely that he isn't. The moon is already sinking,
but not a footstep can be heard, so he may have
changed his mind. If he should not come, . . . I shall
have to live in shame day after day, like a prostitute.
How can I be so lost to shame and evil? For I shall
be no better than a dead body tossed by the roadside.
I shall be dishonored and trampled on, with my shame
brought to light. And yet I shall have to be silent
as if dumb. In that case I shall carry my regret beyond the grave. I'm sure he will come. From the
moment I looked into his eyes when we parted the
other day, that has been my conviction. He is afraid
of me. He hates and despises me, and yet he is afraid
of me. Indeed, if I were to rely only on myself, I
couldn't be sure of him. But I rely on him. I rely
on his selfishness. I rely on the vile fear that selfishness inspires in him.

But now that I can no longer rely on myself, what

a wretched being I am! Until three years ago I had confidence in myself, and above all, in my beauty! It would be more true to say "until that day" than "three years ago." That day when I met him in the room of my aunt's home, a glance into his eyes showed me my ugliness mirrored in his mind. He spoke loving and comforting words to me, looking as if there were nothing the matter. But how can a woman's heart ever be comforted once it has known the ugliness of her own person? I was mortified, horrified, grieved. How much better was the lurid uneasiness of the eclipse of the moon which I saw as a child in my nurse's arms, compared to the ghostly despair that darkened my mind at that moment! All the visions and dreams I had in my heart vanished. The loneliness of a rainy dawn enshrouded me quietly. Shuddering with loneliness, I finally gave up my body, which was as good as dead, into the arms of a man I did not love—into the arms of a lascivious man who hates and despises me. Could I not endure my loneliness since my ugliness was vividly shown to me? Did I try to bury everything in that delirious moment of putting my face on his chest? Or was I moved by mere shameful desire as he was? The mere thought of it overwhelms me with shame! shame! shame! Especially when I took myself from his arms, how ashamed I was.

Vexation and loneliness brought endless tears to my eyes despite my effort not to weep. I was not only grieved because I had been dishonored, I was tortured and pained above all because I was despised like a leprous dog which is hated and tortured. What have I done since then? I have only the vaguest memory of it as if it were a thing of the distant past. I only remember his low voice whispering, "Let's kill Wataru," and his mustache touched my ear as I was sobbing. The instant I heard these words, I felt strangely enlivened. Yes, I felt lively and bright as pale moonlight, if moonlight can be said to be bright. After all, was I not comforted by these words? Oh, am I not—is not a woman a being that feels joy in being loved by a man even if she has to kill her own husband?

I continued to weep for some time with a lonely and lively feeling like moonlight. When did I ever promise to give a helping hand in this murder of my husband?

Not until then had my husband entered my mind. I honestly say "not until then." Until that time my mind was wholly occupied with myself and my dishonor. Then I saw the image of my husband's smiling face. Probably the moment I remembered his face, the plan flashed across my mind. At that time I was already determined to die, and I was glad of my decision. But when I stopped crying, raised my face, and looked up into his own to find my ugliness mirrored in it, I felt as though all my joy had faded out. It reminded me of the darkness of the eclipse of the moon I saw with my nurse. That, as it were, set free at once all the evil spirits lurking under cover of my joy. Is it really because of my love for my husband that I am going to die for him? No, it is merely that under such reasonable pretext, I want to atone for my sin of having slept with another. Having no courage to commit suicide, I have the mean desire to make a good impression on the public. This meanness of mine can perhaps be condoned. Under the pretext of dying for my husband, was I not planning to revenge myself on my lover's hatred of me, his contempt of me, and his wicked lust? This is verified by the fact that a glance into his face put out the mysterious spark of life which is like pale moonlight, and froze my heart with grief. I am going to die not for my husband but for myself. I am going to die to punish my lover's having hurt my heart and for my grudge at his having sullied my body. Oh, not only am I unworthy of living but unworthy of dying.

But now, how much better it is to die even an ignominious death, than to live. Smiling a forced smile, I repeatedly promised to kill my husband with him. Since he is quick-witted, he must have sensed from my words what the consequences would be if he broke his promise. So it seems impossible that after making such a promise he should fall back on it. Is that the sound of the wind? When I think that my afflictions from that day are at last coming to an end tonight, I feel at ease. Tomorrow will not fail to shed its cold light on my headless body. If my husband sees it, he will...no, I won't think of him. My husband loves me. But I have no strength to return his love. I can love only one man. And that very man is coming to kill me tonight. Even this rushlight is too bright for me, tortured by my lover as I am.

Kesa blows out the light. Soon the faint sound of the opening of a shutter is heard, and pale moonlight floods in.

THE DRAGON

"Lord bless me!" said Uji Dainagon Takakuni.*
"Awaking in a dream from my nap, I feel it's especially hot today. Not a breath of wind blows to shake even the wisteria flowers hanging from the pine branch. The murmuring of the spring, which at other times makes me feel cool, is nearly drowned out by the singing of the cicadas, and seems only to add to the sultry heat. Now I will have the servant boys fan me."

"Oh, you say people on the streets have gathered! Then I'll go to. Boys, follow me, and don't forget to bring the big fans.

"Greetings. I'm Takakuni. Pardon the rudeness of my scanty attire.

"Today I have a request to make of you, so I've had my coach stop at the tea-house of Uji. Lately, I've been thinking of coming here to write a story book as others do. But unfortunately I know no stories worth writing. Idle as I am, it bores me to have to rack my brains. So from today I plan to to have you tell me the old stories so that I may put them into a book. Since I, Takakuni, am always

---

* *Uji Dainagon Takakuni* (1087–1160). 'Dainagon' was the government office of Chief Councilor of State in olden days. Uji Takakuni, the author of 'Konjaku Monogatari,' has been traditionally, though not authentically, identified with the author of 'the Uji Shuishu ('Gleanings from the Tales of Uji'), from which Akutagawa took this story.

around and about the Imperial Court, I shall be able
to collect from all quarters many unusual anecdotes
and curious stories. So you, good folks, troublesome
though it may be, will you grant my request?

"You all grant my request? A thousand thanks!
Then I will listen to your stories one by one."

"Here, boys. Start using your big fans so that
the whole room may have a breeze. That will make
us a little cooler. You, ironmaster, and you potter,
don't be reserved. Both of you, step nearer to this
desk. That woman who sells '*sushi*,'* if the sunlight
is too hot for you, you'd better put your pail in a
corner of the verandah. Priest, lay down your golden
hand-drum. You, samurai, and you, mountain priest,
there, have you spread your mats?

"Are you all ready? Then if you're ready, potter,
since you are the oldest, you first tell us any story
you prefer."

"We are greatly obliged for your courteous greet-
ing," the old man replied. "Your Lordship graciously said that you would make a story book of what
we humble folks are going to tell you. This is a far
greater honor than I deserve. But if I should decline,
Your Lordship wouldn't be pleased. So I'll take the
liberty of telling you a foolish old story. It may be
somewhat tiresome, but please listen to my tale for
a while."

The old man began his story.

* *sushi.* Boiled rice flavored with vinegar, often pressed into
balls, and served with fish, fried eggs, etc.

THE DRAGON

In old days when I was quite young, in Nara there lived a priest called Kurodo Tokugyo who had an extraordinarily large nose. The tip of his nose shone frightfully crimson all the year round, as if it'd been stung by a wasp. So the people of Nara nicknamed him Ohana-no Kurodo Tokugyo.* But because that name was too long, they came to call him Hanazō.** I myself saw him a couple of times in the Kofuku Temple in Nara. He had such a fine red nose that I, too, thought that he might well be scornfully called Hanazo.

On a certain night, Hanazo, that is, Ohana-no Kurodo Tokugyo, the priest, came alone to the pond of Sarusawa, without the company of his disciples, and set up, on the bank in front of the weeping willow, a notice-board which said in bold characters, "On March third a dragon shall ascend from this pond." But as a matter of fact, he didn't know whether or not a dragon really lived in the pond of Sarusawa, and needless to say, the dragon's ascension to heaven on March third was a black lie. It would have been more certain if he had said that no dragon would ascend to heaven. The reason why he made such needless mischief is that he was displeased with the priests of Nara who were habitually making fun of his nose, and he planned to play a trick on them this

* Ohana-no Kurodo Tokugyo. '*Ohana*' means a big nose. '*Kurodo*' means an official in the Imperial Archives. '*Tokugyo*' might mean a person accomplished in religious austerities.
** Hanazo might mean a big-nosed fellow.

89

time and laugh at them to his heart's content. Your Lordship must think it quite ridiculous. But this is an old story, and in those days people who played such tricks were by no means uncommon.

The next day, the first to find this notice-board was an old woman who came to worship Buddha at the Kofuku Temple every morning. When she neared the still misty pond, leaning on a bamboo cane with her rosary in her hand, she found the notice-board, which she had not seen under the weeping-willow the day before. She wondered why a board announcing a Buddhist mass should stand in such a strange place. But since she could not read any of the characters, she was about to pass it by, when she fortunately met a robed priest coming from the opposite direction, and she had him read it for her. The notice said, "On March third a dragon shall ascend from this pond." They were astonished at this.

The old woman was amazed. Stretching her bent body, she looked up into the priest's face and asked, "Is it possible that a dragon lives in this pond?" The priest assumed an air of still more composure and said to her, "In former times a certain Chinese scholar had a lump over his eye-lid which itched terribly. One day the sky suddenly became overcast, and a thunder shower rained down in torrents. Then instantly his lump burst and a dragon is said to have ascended straight up to heaven trailing a cloud. Since a dragon could live even in a lump, tens of dragons

90

could naturally live at the bottom of a big pond like this." With these words he expounded the matter to her. The old woman, who had always been convinced that a priest never lied, was astounded out of her wits, and said, "I see. Now that you mention it, the color of the water over there does look suspicious." Although it was not yet March third, she hurried away, scarcely bothering to use her cane, panting out her Buddhist prayers, and leaving the priest behind alone.

Had it not been for the people about him, the priest would have split his sides with laughter. This was only natural, for the priest was none other than the author of the notice-board, that is, Kurodo Tokugyo, nicknamed Hanazo. He had been walking about the pond with the preposterous idea that some gullible persons might be caught by the notice-board which he put up the night before. After the old woman left, he found an early traveler accompanied by a servant who carried her burden on his back. She had a skirt with a design of insects on it, and was reading the notice-board from beneath her sedgehat. Then the priest cautiously stifling his laugh with great effort, stood in front of the sign, pretending to read it. After giving a sniff with his red nose, he slowly went back toward the Kofuku Temple. Then, in front of the big southern gate of the temple, by chance he met the priest called Emon ,who lived in the same cell as he himself.

"You are up unusually early today," Emon said,

furrowing his dark, thick, stubborn brow. "The weather may change."

"The weather may really change," Hanazo readily replied with a knowing look, dilating his nose. "I'm told that a dragon will ascend to heaven from the Sarusawa Pond on March third."

Hearing this, Emon glared dubiously at Hanazo. But soon purring in his throat, he said with a sardonic smile, "You had a good dream, I suppose. I was once told that to dream of a dragon ascending to heaven is an auspicious omen." So saying he tried to go past Hanazo, tossing his mortar-shaped head. But he must have heard Hanazo muttering to himself, "A lost soul is beyond redemption." Turning back with such hateful force that the supports of his hemp-thonged clogs bent for the moment, he demanded of Hanazo, in a tone as vehement as if he would challenge him to a Buddhist controversy, "Is there any positive proof that a dragon will ascend to heaen?"

Thereupon, Hanazo, affecting perfect composure, pointed towards the pond, on which the sun was already beginning to shed its light, and replied, looking down at him, "If you doubt my remark, you ought to see the notice-board in front of the weeping-willow."

Obstinate as Emon was, his normal keen reasoning must have lost a little of its initial impetuosity. Blindly, as if his eyes were dazzled, he asked in a half-hearted voice, "Well, has such a notice-board been set up?" and went off in a thoughtful mood, with his mortar-shaped head to one side.

You may well imagine how this amused Hanazo, who saw him going away. He felt the whole of his red nose itch, and while he went up the stone-steps of the big southern gate with a sullen expression, he could not help bursting into laughter in spite of himself.

Even that first morning the notice-board saying "On March third a dragon shall ascend" had a great effect on the public. In the course of a day or two the dragon in the pond of Sarusawa became the talk of the whole town of Nara. Of course some said, "The notice-board may be somebody's hoax." Also at that time there spread in Kyoto a rumor that the dragon in the Shinsen-en had ascended to heaven. Even those who asserted that the prophecy on the notice-board was a hoax started to waver between belief and doubt as to the truth of the rumor, and began to think that such an event might possibly occur.

Just then an unexpected wonder took place. Less than ten days later the nine year old daughter of a certain Shinto priest who served the Shrine of Kasuga was drowsing, with her head in her mother's lap, when a black dragon fell like a cloud from heaven, and said in human speech, "At last I am to ascend to heaven on March third. But rest at ease, since I expect to cause no trouble to you townspeople." The moment she woke up, she told her mother about her dream. The talk that the little girl had dreamt of the dragon in the pond of Sarusawa caused a great sensation in the town. The story was exaggerated in one way and another: a child possessed of a dragon wrote a poem, a dragon appeared to such and such a shrine priest in a dream and gave him a divine revelation.

In the course of time, one man went so far as to say that he had actually seen a dragon, although no dragon could be expected even to have thrust his head above water. He was an old man who went to the market to sell fish every morning. At dawn one day he came to the pond of Sarusawa. Through the morning haze he saw the wide expanse of water gleam with a faint light under the bank where the weeping-willow stood and where the notice-board was set up. At any rate it was the time when the rumor of the dragon was on everyone's lips. So he thought that the dragon god had come out. Trembling all over with this half happy and half dreadful thought, he left his catch of river fish there, and stealing up, he held on to the weeping-willow and tried to look into the pond. Then he saw an unknown monster like a coiled black chain lurking ominously at the bottom of the faintly illuminated water. Probably frightened by human foot-steps, the dreadful monster, uncoiled and disappeared somewhere in a twinkling. At this sight the man broke into a cold sweat, and returned to the place where he had left his fish, only to find that a score of fish, including some carp and eels which he was carrying to the market, had disappeared. Some laughed at this rumor, saying, "He was probably deceived by an old otter." But not a few said, "Since it's impossible for an otter to live in the pond which the dragon king rules and protects, the dragon king took pity on the life of the fish, and must have called them down into the pond where he lives."

In the meantime, the notice-board message "On March third a dragon shall ascend from this pond," came to be more and more talked about, and Hanazo elated by this success, chuckled to himself, and dilated his nose. Time went on and the third of March drew near. Four or five days before the scheduled ascension of the dragon, to Hanazo's great astonishment, his aunt, a priestess in Sakurai in the province of Settsu, came up all the long way to Nara, saying that she wanted by all means to see the dragon's ascension. He was quite embarrassed, and resorted to frightening, coaxing and a thousand other means, to persuade her to go back to Sakurai. But she obstinately refused and stayed on without listening to his advice, saying, "I'm very old. If I can have a glimpse of the dragon king and worship him, I shall be happy to die." He could not now confess that out of mischief he himself had put up the notice-board. At last Hanazo yielded, and not only did he agree to take care of her until March third, but he had to promise her that he would accompany her to see the dragon god's ascension on the day.

Since even his aunt, the priestess, had heard of the dragon, the rumor must have spread to the province of Settsu, Izumi, and Kawachi, and possibly as far as to the provinces of Harima, Yamashiro, Omi and Tamba, to say nothing of the province of Yamato. The mischief he had done with the intention of playing a trick upon the people of Nara had brought about the unexpected result of deceiving tens of thousands of people in many provinces. When he thought of this, he felt more alarmed than pleased. While he was showing his aunt, the priestess, around the temples of Nara every day, he had the guilty conscience of a criminal hiding out of the sight of the police commissioner. But while on one hand he felt uneasy when he learned from hearsay on the streets that incense had been burnt and flowers offered before the notice-board, on the other, he felt as happy as if he had accomplished some great achievement.

Days passed by, and at last came the third of March, when the dragon was to ascend to heaven.

As his promise left him no alternative, he reluctantly accompanied his aunt to the top of the stone steps of the big southern gate of the Kofuku Temple, which commanded a bird's-eye view of the pond of Sarusawa. It was a clear and cloudless day, and there was not a breath of wind to ring even a wind-bell at a gate.

The spectators who had been looking forward to the day thronged in from the provinces of Kawachi, Izumi, Settsu, Harima, Yamashiro, Omi, Tamba and others, to say nothing of the city of Nara. Looking out from the top of the stone steps, he saw, as far as the eye could reach, a sea of people stretching in all directions to the end of the thoroughfare of Nijo in the hazy distance. All kinds of ceremonial head-gear rustled in waves. Here and there ox-carts, elaborately decorated with blue or red tassels or in tasteful shades, towered over the mass of people, their roofs inlaid with gold and silver shining dazzlingly in the beautiful spring sunlight. Some people had put up sunshades, some pitched flat tents, others set up elaborate stands on the streets. The area in the vicinity of the pond, spread out under his eyes, presented a scene reminiscent of the Kamo festival, although out of season. Priest Hanazo who now saw this, had little dreamt that setting up a mere notice-board would cause such great excitement.

"What tremendous crowds of people!" Hanazo said in a feeble voice, looking back at his aunt as in great amazement. And he squatted down at the foot of the column of the large southern gate, apparently without even the spirit to sniff with his large nose.

But his aunt, the priestess, was far from able to read his innermost thoughts. Stretching out her neck so far that her hood almost slipped off, she looked around here and there, and chattered continually, "Indeed, the view of the pond where the dragon king lives is exquisite. Since such big crowds have turned out, the dragon god will be sure to appear, won't he?" and so on.

Hanazo could not keep on squatting at the foot of the column, so reluctantly he stood up, to find a large crowd of people in creased or triangular ceremonial head-gear on the stone steps. Then in the crowd, who did he recognize but Priest Emon looking intently toward the pond, with his mortar-shaped head towering conspicuously above the others. At this sight he suddenly forgot his wretched feeling. Amused and tickled by the idea that he had taken in even this fellow, he called out to him, "Priest," and asked him mockingly, "Are you here also to see the dragon's ascension?"

"Yes," Emon replied, looking backward arrogantly. Then, assuming an unusually serious look, his dark thick eyebrows growing rigid, he added, "He is slow in coming out."

Hanazo felt that the trick had overreached itself and his buoyant voice sank, and he looked vacantly down over a sea of people, as helpless as ever. But although a long time passed, there were no indications of the dragon ascending in the limpid surface of the water, which apparently had already become slightly warmer, mirroring distinctly the cherries and willows on the bank. Probably because masses of spectators were crowded for miles around, the pond today seemed smaller than usual, furthering impression that there could be no dragon.

But all the spectators waited patiently with breathless interest as if unconscious of the passage of hours. The sea of people under the gate spread wider and wider. As time went on, the ox-carts became so numerous that in some places their axles jostled one another. It may well be imagined from the preceding account how miserable Hanazo felt at this sight. But then a strange thing happened, for Hanazo began to feel in his heart that a dragon was really likely to ascend—at first, he began to feel that it might not be impossible for a dragon to ascend. Of course he was the author of the notice-board, and he ought not to have entertained any such absurd idea. But while he was looking at the surging of the ceremonial head-gear, he actually began to feel that some such alarming event might happen.

This may have been because the excitement of the multitude of people impressed Hanazo without his being aware of it. Or it may be that he felt guilty when he thought over the fact that his trick caused such great general excitement, and that without being aware of it, he began to desire in his heart, that a dragon should really ascend from the pond. Whatever the reason, his miserable feeling gradually faded away, though he knew quite well that it was he himself who had written the sentence on the notice-board, and he too began gazing at the surface of the pond as intently as his aunt. Indeed, had he not conceived such a fancy, he could not have remained standing under the large southern gate all day long, waiting for the impossible ascension of the dragon.

But the pond of Sarusawa, not a ripple rising, reflected back the spring sunlight. The sky was bright and clear with not a speck of cloud floating. Still the spectators, as closely packed as ever under sunshades and flat tents and behind the balustrades of stands, awaited the appearance of the dragon king in the throes of expectation, as if they had been unaware of the passage of time from morning to noon and from noon to evening.

Nearly half a day had gone by since Hanazo had arrived there. Then a streak of cloud like the smoke of a joss stick trailed in mid-air. Suddenly it grew larger and larger, and the sky which had been bright and clear became dusky. At that moment a gust of wind swept down over the pond and ruffled the glassy surface of the water into innumerable waves. Then in the twinkling of an eye, white rain came down in torrents before the spectators, prepared as they were, had time to scurry helter-skelter. Furthermore, terrific claps of thunder suddenly pealed, and flashes of lightning flew past one another like wefts of a fabric. Then hooked hands seemed to tear apart a cluster of clouds, and in the excess of their force they raised a spout of water over the pond. At that instant Hanazo's eyes caught a blurred vision of a black dragon more than one hundred feet long ascending straight into the sky, with its golden talons flashing. But this happened in a twinkling. After that, amidst a storm, cherry blossoms around the pond were seen flying up into the dusky sky. It hardly need be said that the disconcerted spectators, as they scurried away, formed waves of humanity which surged like the waves in the pond.

Eventually the torrential rain stopped and a blue

sky began to peep through the clouds. Then Hanazo stared around him as if he had forgotten his large nose. Was the figure of the dragon which he had just seen an illusion? While he wondered, author of the notice-board as he was, he began to feel that the dragon's ascension was impossible. Nevertheless, he did actually see it. So, the more he thought over the event, the more mysterious it became. At that time, when he raised his aunt, who had been lying more dead than alive at the foot of the column near by, he was unable to conceal his bewilderment and fright. He asked her timidly, "Did you see the dragon?" His aunt, who had been stunned for a time, heaved a great sigh, and could do nothing but repeat her nod in fear. Presently in a trembling voice she answered, "Surely I did. Wasn't he a dragon, black all over, with only his golden talons flashing?"

So probably it was not only the eyes of Hanazo, or Kurodo Tokugyo, who saw the dragon. Yes, later it was said that most of the people of all ages and sexes who had been there on that day had seen the black dragon ascending to heaven in a dark cloud.

Later Hanazo confessed that the notice-board had been his own mischievous idea. But I am told none of his fellow-priests, not even Emon, believed his confession. Now did his notice-board hit the mark? Or did it miss? Ask Hanazo or Kurodo Tokugyo the Big Nosed, and probably he himself will be unable to reply to this question.

"What a mysterious story, indeed!" said Uji-

Dainagon Takakuni. "In the old days a dragon seems to have lived in that pond of Sarusawa. What! You cannot tell whether it did even in the old days? Yes, in the old days it must have lived there. In those times all people believed that dragons lived at the bottom of water. So, naturally, dragons ought to have flown between heaven and earth and at times ought to have appeared in mysterious forms like gods. But I would rather hear your stories than make my comments. The next story is the itinerant priest's turn, isn't it?"

"What?" Takakuni went on. "Is your story about a long-nosed priest called Ikeno-no-Zenchinaigu? That will be all the more interesting following the story of Hanazo. Now tell it to me at once..."

Other Titles in the Tuttle Library